PRAISE FOR

UNCOVERING THE **MYSTERIES** OF GOD

To be human is to struggle with the "whys" of life.
Jeff Kinley helps us acknowledge that struggle and invites
us into honest, street-level conversation. Whether you are
a person of deep faith or one who is on a spiritual quest,
you will find yourself in Kinley's dialogue. More important,
you will find a limitless, mysterious God who engages
with you, heart, soul, body and mind.

Sally Morgenthaler
Author and Speaker
www.trueconversations.com

I consider Jeff one of my dear friends. He has an amazing
ability to communicate, whether on paper or in person.
For a generation that needs to be met right where they are,
Jeff has a gift of reaching people on their level without
compromising depth or truth.

Bart Millard
Lead Singer, MercyMe

UNCOVERING THE
MYSTERIES
OF GOD

JEFF KINLEY
Co-author of *I Can Only Imagine*

Regal

From Gospel Light
Ventura, California, U.S.A.

Published by Regal
From Gospel Light
Ventura, California, U.S.A.
www.regalbooks.com
Printed in the U.S.A.

Published in association with William K. Jensen Literary Agency, Eugene, Oregon.

Library of Congress Cataloging-in-Publication Data
Kinley, Jeff.
  Uncovering the mysteries of God / Jeff Kinley.
    p. cm.
  Includes bibliographical references.
  ISBN 978-0-8307-4425-1 (trade paper)
  1. Mystery. 2. God (Christianity) I. Title.
  BT127.5.K56 2007
  230–dc22

                                                                    2007021807

                    1 2 3 4 5 6 7 8 9 10 / 10 09 08 07

Rights for publishing this book outside the U.S.A. or in non-English languages are administered by Gospel Light Worldwide, an international not-for-profit ministry. For additional information, please visit www.glww.org, email info@glww.org, or write to Gospel Light Worldwide, 1957 Eastman Avenue, Ventura, CA 93003, U.S.A.

*Dedicated to those I am privileged to
pastor at Vintagenxt Church.
Travelers together on this mysterious
journey (see Psalm 71:18).*

CONTENTS

It was the experience of mystery—even if mixed with fear—
that engendered religion.

Albert Einstein, "The World As I See It"

ACKNOWLEDGMENTS

Behind every successful author there is a hard-working agent. While one is pounding the keyboard, the other is pounding the pavement. As my agent, Bill Jensen represents me well, and I am very grateful for his diligence, insight and the ability to keep his finger on the pulse of the publishing industry.

Thanks to Alex Field at Regal for recognizing the potential for this book, and a special thanks to the behind-the-scene professionals at Regal whose work often goes unrecognized.

A big credit goes to my creative wife, Beverly, for initially suggesting the concept for this book. And thanks to my son Stuart, who came up with the original title.

And finally, to my friends at our neighborhood coffee house (a.k.a. my "office"), for keeping my coffee cup full and allowing me to transform table #56 into a writing desk.

THE FRONT DOOR

I live in a very mysterious house. Located in a historic district of
Little Rock, Arkansas, it's a big old home with trapdoors, secret
rooms and multiple staircases—four stories if you count the
attic. And because of its size, there are places in my house where,
if you scream, no one will hear you. We have rooms filled with
pre-Civil War furniture. There are doors that creak and unexplained noises throughout. We've uncovered hidden artifacts
and walled-up relics, remnants of past lives long since erased
from memory. There's always something to find in the wall or
under the floor when we remodel. There have been unpleasant
surprises too, like the time water poured from the ceiling of my
study or when a small creek flowed under the basement. But
these revelations haven't always been disastrous. The objects
we've uncovered have led us to a greater understanding of our
84-year-old home and opened a window into the lives of those
who preceded us here. With each new discovery, we travel back
in time. We discover forgotten trinkets and treasures, some that
we're quite sure were never meant to be found.

It's a house with many stories to tell. Sometimes those tales
are short and simple. Other times we only find a fragment of
the truth, with most of the puzzle pieces still missing. That's
when the real mystery kicks in. And it's during those times that
we have to connect the dots in order to make some sense of it

all. Who hid a World War II mortar shell in the attic and why? And what's the meaning of the eerie recording we found concealed in a ceiling? Why did a music box unexpectedly play on its own? Who was that woman whose photograph we discovered buried within a basement wall? Was she a family member? A houseguest? A mistress? A person whose identity was intended to be forever secret?

The mysteries of our spacious Tudor-style home continue to this day. Who can tell what we'll find next? We don't have all the answers or all the whys. But we're content to live in a house of the known, unknown and the *not-yet*-known.

Oddly, I find that my *faith* shares a lot of similarities with my *home*: mysterious, puzzling, mystifying and even baffling. There are times when God stuff is simple and clear to me, but every now and then, it can be about as clear as the murky waters of the nearby Arkansas River. It's these *unknowns* of my faith that confound and often confuse me. Occasionally, upon further investigation, the waters clear and I understand what was once confusing. But there are other mysteries about God and the Christian faith that continue to haunt me—stuff I am still exploring and trying to make sense of.

Maybe you know what I'm talking about. If so, then take a stroll with me through some of these mysteries. Think of it as a walking tour of a big old house. Each room is a mystery. Each door, a passageway opening up new adventures. But be prepared for a few trapdoors, hidden compartments, buried artifacts, disturbing noises and maybe even a leaky roof or two.

These mysteries aren't your typical formula-driven fiction found in the pages of dollar-store paperbacks. They're more real than classic Sherlock Holmes. More riveting than a who-dunit movie. More graphic than *CSI Miami*. These are the stories of brain-bending paradoxes, sealed books and secret meetings, demonic hosts and deadly curses, hidden treasures and hounding visitors.

Some of these mysteries will amaze you. Others will confuse you. Perhaps perplex you. Maybe even upset you. Some of them unfold slowly, like sunlight at dawn. Others may keep you in the dark for longer than you'd like. Some of them are deceiving. At first glance, you might think you already have the mystery solved. But then there's a twist in the story line, something that causes you to put the book down and think for a few minutes, maybe even longer. The mystery will elude you for a while. But if you keep searching and sleuthing, you may find what you're looking for. Some are simple truths often complicated through misunderstanding. Some of these mysteries are so simple, they're easy to miss. Some are so deep, you can quickly get lost in the abyss. But you'll soon learn that from time to time it's okay to get lost.

These are some of the classic riddles of mankind. Ancient secrets, hidden for hundreds, even thousands of years. But you'll have to look at the clues and personally examine the evidence that lies in your path. There are signs and hints all along the way. The truth you'll uncover through these mysteries will do more than just open your eyes. It will illumine your mind. These mysteries will bring you face to face with wisdom. Wisdom from the ages. Wisdom *for* the ages. Wisdom for *you*.

If you're looking for quick answers or nicely packaged, neat theological explanations for these mysteries, then you'll have to look somewhere else.

But if you're hungry for honest dialogue about why your faith seems so hazy, you'll find a mother lode of treasure here and a journey into the mystery of God Himself.

No, it's not a pot of gold or a suitcase of cash hidden under the stairs.

It's something a whole lot better.

Jeff Kinley
Little Rock, Arkansas

CHAPTER 1

A BRILLIANT PLAN

THE MYSTERY OF THE GOD-MAN

The mystery of God, namely, Christ.

Colossians 2:2

William is scared. Scared to *death*. Terrified. His breathing grows shallow as his pulse accelerates. He can almost hear his own heartbeat now.

It's that rare moment in life few of us ever really experience—that moment right before death when a flood of thoughts and memories flash in your brain like a fourth of July fireworks show. Thoughts of home. Memories of family. Question marks about life and whether yours has really been worth it. Emotions race across the horizon of your soul like a herd of wild buffalo. Alarm bells are sounding. Paranoia presses against your brain. Insecurity and uncertainty blanket your heart. And fear haunts you like an invisible monster.

Most of us have never known the kind of terror William is experiencing. Few of us ever will. Oh, we identify with the occasional jump scare from an unexpected person appearing from behind us. Perhaps you're familiar with that sudden jolt of adrenaline that races down your back during a frightening scene in a movie. Maybe that few-second-scare you get on a roller coaster faintly resembles what I'm talking about. But that's *fun* fear, isn't it? You almost *enjoy* being scared that way.

This is different. Completely different. William's fear is a sudden shock to the nervous system that sends all his faculties into emergency preservation mode. More than a moment of fright, it's a kind of ultimate, paralyzing dread. A fear factor way beyond what you see rehearsed on network television. It's a brand of fear that sets its claws into him, taking up permanent residence in his mind. It's terror as a constant companion. It's a nagging headache throbbing in his skull.

A terror of the soul.

That's what William is facing. With the barrel of a rifle pointed just inches from his stomach and a nervous finger on the trigger, he's unsure he'll live to see another sunrise.

It's November 4, 1979. William Daugherty is a newly arrived member of America's embassy staff in Tehran, Iran. On this day, the embassy is suddenly stormed by hundreds of radical Islamic students, seizing the American compound by force. Overcome and outnumbered by militant extremists, the Marine guard assigned to the compound have no choice but to surrender their posts. Iran is a nation in mid-revolution, a country in chaos, and these attacking militants are protesting the "Great Satan's" involvement in Iran's government affairs. An international crisis was touched off when U.S. President Jimmy Carter refused to turn over Iran's former authoritarian leader, the Shah, to stand trial in his own country. And now, 52 Americans have been taken hostage. William is caught in the middle of this political predicament. Unknown to him, his terrifying ordeal has only just begun.

Much later, following months of failed negotiations and economic sanctions against Iran, President Carter issued an executive order authorizing a covert military rescue attempt. After months of tactical planning with some of the nation's top covert military strategists, a plan was proposed and approved. But for an operation of this magnitude to work, it would have to be executed flawlessly, with surgical precision. There would be no room for failure. No margin of error. Nothing left to chance.

The first stage of this secret mission called for establishing a small staging area in the Great Salt Desert of eastern Iran. Code-named Desert One, this area, some 256 miles south of the capital city of Tehran, would serve as a temporary airstrip for the transport planes and helicopters. After refueling the aircraft, ground troops would board the helicopters and fly near Tehran. Then, after locating and extracting the hostages from the embassy, they would be airlifted to a base outside of the city, where C-130 transports would safely bring them out of the country under the protection of American fighter aircraft.

The president hoped for a quick operation utilizing tactical surprise and accuracy. An incisive insertion. Get in. Raid the compound. Safely extract the hostages. Get out. Come home. Done deal. It was a brilliant plan, called the most "complex amphibious raid in military history."

On the night of April 24, 1980, with every piece of the strategic rescue puzzle in place, an assault force of 139 Army Special Operations Forces soldiers boarded their respective aircraft for the stealth night mission. The USS Coral Sea sat 58 miles off the Iranian coastline, ready to provide fighter coverage and air support. A small advance team had already infiltrated Tehran to conduct a visual reconnaissance of the embassy area and to secure ground transportation.

At 7:05 P.M. local time, eight Marine helicopters left the USS Nimitz for their 600-nautical-mile journey into the desert, using night-vision goggles and flying just 100 feet above the ground. Once the helicopters refueled at Desert One, this brilliant rescue attempt known as Operation Eagle Claw would be in full swing. The good guys were on their way.

They never made it.

What was, on paper, a brilliant plan went from covert to catastrophic.

Just 140 miles into their mission, one of the Sea Stallion helicopters was forced to land after warning lights indicated a cracked rotor blade. Following this, two more helicopters went down well short of their rendezvous site, due to an unexpected sandstorm. A third helicopter was damaged on landing at Desert One. The situation was not good.

Now with a shortage of aircraft, the clandestine operation was put in serious jeopardy. After consultation at the highest command level, the difficult decision to abort the mission was made. The troops would have to return home empty-handed. There would be no rescue for William and his fellow hostages. No release from captivity. No end to their suffering, torture and terror. Their deliverance would have to wait. Operation Eagle Claw had failed to make history. Now it *was* history.

Almost.

Tragically, as Special Forces exited their makeshift desert runway, a helicopter clipped a C-130, crashed and exploded, killing eight American servicemen and injuring four more. The remaining troops were quickly loaded onto the other aircraft and beat a hasty retreat into the desert night. All that remained of the covert operation was eight dead bodies and a huge charred spot in the sand.

Now the captives weren't the only ones suffering. Grieving with them were the families of the brave soldiers who gave their lives in the rescue attempt. And the United States, along with her world-famous might and military intelligence, suffered global embarrassment and criticism. So did President Carter, who soundly lost his reelection campaign only a few months later. In the end, the American hostages were held prisoner for

444 days, finally being released within minutes of Ronald Reagan's inauguration.

History now remembers Operation Eagle Claw as a very good plan gone very wrong.

"Heaven, We Have a Problem"

Let's consider another hostage crisis. A very different kind. This one doesn't occur in the Middle East but right here where you and I live. It's not about 52 Americans held hostage by a revolutionary regime but about Americans and Iranians held hostage by another terrorist government. Instead of a president, a much higher power is involved, and there's a much more serious problem. This time, the stakes are higher and more personal. And it involves a covert rescue operation more mysterious than any you could possibly imagine.

Here's the background: Through a really bad choice, the first humans revolted against their Creator, igniting an explosion of global selfishness—also known as the *S* word—sin. This detonation sent aftershocks rippling throughout history. Ironically, with each new generation, the fallout from this blast becomes worse. Look at our world and maybe you'll agree. We're *way* off course here, drifting in nothingness. A planet lost in space. Damaged beyond repair. Desperate, we've scavenged scraps from humanity's junkyard, trying to patch up the hole left by our decision to leave God. We've tried everything, but we keep coming up empty. We've searched *within* ourselves looking for a way to rewrite our sad story—meditation, mysticism, man-made religion—but nothing works.

We've probed outer space with massive telescopes, looking for that elusive contact with extraterrestrial life. With satellite dishes the size of small towns, we've scanned the heavens, searching for anything that might help make sense of our nonsensical existence. But apart from inspiring some really cool sci-fi movies, the silence of outer space has been deafening. No one seems to be listening.

But here's where the mystery takes an unexpected turn. The Creator didn't wait around for His creation to cry out to Him about our problem. He knows we're too proud to do that. So *He* did something instead. He got personally involved in this thing before our first parents had the chance to sabotage humanity.

Imagine way back—before humans, Earth, galaxies, space and time—somewhere a gazillion years ago. Before *anything*, the Father, Son and Holy Spirit gathered for a secret meeting. Of course, an all-knowing God doesn't need to problem-solve in a board meeting, right? But bear with me for a minute.

Father: We are perfect and sinless and cannot allow sin-scarred creatures into heaven. Further, Our righteous character requires that We punish sin.

Son: Humankind, the crown of Our creation, is unable to rescue themselves from their problem.

Spirit: They would have to be clothed in Our perfection in order for Us to have relationship with them.

Father: We must conceive of a plan, something that only God can accomplish, something humankind could never do for themselves. If humankind is to escape retribution, One of Us must receive the punishment for sin in their place. One of Us must suffer for those on Earth. One of Us must take on humanity.

Spirit: I will perform the miracle needed for this to happen.

Son: I will go.

Okay, that conversation makes me dizzy. And I'm not suggesting that solving mankind's mysterious sin problem is some kind of theological math equation:

$$humanity - sin + holiness = heaven$$

But God is faced with a complex hurdle here. Humans are hostage to sin, enslaved to a cruel master ultimately more terrifying than any militant religious group. So the Creator creates a masterful rescue strategy. Out of His mysterious collective intellect comes a plan so strange and unconventional that it must have caused the angels to scratch their heads in celestial confusion. Remarkably, this plan calls for the Father to punish the Son for humankind's sin problem (which causes me to scratch my head!). And somehow He will do all this without ever ceasing to be God. We're talking about some bizarre stuff here that is way past the deep end of the pool, way beyond any theologian's ability to figure out.

Maybe that's why it's called a mystery.

At the core of the mystery is this: How could God become a man? How could we ever *see* the invisible God? I mean, how could a God who dwells in unapproachable light and holiness get sweaty and dirty? How could a God who is supposed to be everywhere be confined to one body and one place at a time? How and why would a God who is continually worshiped by an inestimable number of angels give up that adoration for even one minute?

Why indeed?

The Plan

To begin exploring this mystery, let's rewind time and rendez-vous with a young Jewish girl named Mary. Her story, as you probably know, is unique. Minding her own business, she one day encounters an unexpected visitor who turns out to be an angel named Gabriel (see Luke 1:26-38).

This angel drops the first clue in our God-Man mystery. He tells Mary that the Most High will become a man, born like everybody else—through a woman. A bigger surprise comes when Mary learns this woman is *her*! The news is both confusing and frightening, especially to a young girl. But then the good news: Mary's son will be the Savior of the world, the One for whom they have been waiting for centuries. Mary probably already believed in a coming Messiah, but she would have been hard-pressed to explain the idea of a miracle baby.

It's a colossal concept for me to grasp, and I live in a generation that is not easily impressed or wowed. What then, was it like for a first-century teenage girl to swallow? Imagine the dilemma young Mary faced: First, she's engaged and will have some serious explaining to do when she tells her fiancé this "good news." Second, and even more perplexing, Mary is still a virgin!

Umm . . . excuse me, Mr. Angel? . . . Sir? Okay, I know I'm really young, but I am old enough to know how people have babies. Did I miss something in the birds and bees talk? How do I become pregnant without sex? [Mary actually says, "How will this be . . . since I am a virgin?" (Luke 1:34).]

Mary cannot possibly *conceive* (pun intended) how a virgin could remain a virgin and yet become pregnant. So Gabriel explains it:

The Holy Spirit will come upon you, and the power of the Most High will overshadow you. So the holy one to be born will be called the Son of God. . . . nothing is impossible with God (Luke 1:25-27).

And Mary responds, "Great! I get it now. Thanks for making it so simple."

I don't think so.

My guess is that she walked away more confused than ever before. How could a baby just appear inside her, be born like any other baby and yet be unlike any other baby? How could Mary be sinful but her baby be sinless, morally perfect in every way? How could the infinite Second Member of the Godhead enter the confines of time and space, clothe Himself as an infant and grow up like every other human? How could this baby be 100-percent man and 100-percent God?

Without clear answers to any of these important questions, Mary is fully aware that she risks a broken engagement, public humiliation and possibly even death (see Deut. 22:23-24).

Think about it, ladies. You're sworn to be faithful and pure to your fiancé, and you're about to become pregnant through a miracle of God. After a few months, when it's obvious you're great with child, who's going to believe that you still haven't had sex, that you're still a virgin? And what about when you explain to them that your baby is the Son of God? You think anybody (including your parents) will believe you? Can you understand why few people bought her story?

Visualize the impact of this pregnancy on Mary's reputation. Imagine the rumors spread by whispering women and snickering men. Are you willing to say yes to God and endure all this? Willing to trash your good name in the community? To shame your husband before the Temple priests and elders of the city? Willing to gamble all that away with one roll of the dice? Willing to live with the fact that people will always suspect that you and Joseph cooked up this wild story to cover up your premarital sexual escapade? Are you willing to risk being dragged out to the city gate to be brutally executed by an angry mob? Mary, have you really thought through all this?

Embracing this mystery was no easy assignment. And though she was young, Mary understood that the stakes were high. Yet her reply?

"I am the Lord's servant," Mary answered. "May it be to me as you have said." Then the angel left her (Luke 1:38).

Just like that, Mary puts her trust in God's mysterious proposal to save mankind. I suspect she still suffered from bouts of confusion, ignorance and awe. Nevertheless, the plan goes into action. As expected, Mary's fiancé, Joseph, doesn't believe her at first and thinks to divorce her—secretly though, for her protection. His heart is understandably broken by this supposed betrayal. That is, until an angel visits him one night and informs him of God's involvement. Like Mary, Joseph accepts his role, risking the same public scandal, shame and ridicule. Now *that's* love . . . and *faith.*

Is this blowing your mind yet?

The Mission

No credible historian disputes the fact of Jesus' birth. How He got here and what He did is another story. So-called scholars cast doubt on the likelihood of a virgin-born boy growing up to be the Son of God. But supposing there really is a God . . . anything is possible, including a virgin birth, right?

The Bible claims Mary had her Son exactly as Gabriel had predicted. Not much is known about Jesus' childhood or adolescence. For us, it becomes the mysterious missing chapter of His life. Maybe that's because the really important parts of God's plan kicked in when Jesus was 30. As it turns out, His reasons for becoming a man are made clear to us during those final three years. Solving the mystery of the God-Man is seen not only through *how* He came (the virgin birth) but also through *why* He came:

> For God so loved the world that he gave his only begotten Son, that whoever believes in him should not perish but have eternal life (John 3:16).

God gave us His Son, arguably the greatest Gift ever given by anyone to anybody. But I suspect this mystery can be better understood by grasping His mission. The following keys will help us unlock hidden doors leading to the real story.

Show and Tell

Beau is a good friend of mine, though we haven't always been close. We first met a few years back when his daughter was part of a group I took to England. We had only occasional contact at first, but during the past two years we've reconnected in a more meaningful way, meeting regularly at a local coffee shop. Sipping the daily brew, we talk about our families, ministry, manhood, music—virtually everything. But something better than that has happened over the last few months. The more Beau and I talked, the more I learned about him, and vice-versa. The more he opened up about his life, the better I understood him. I now know things about Beau I didn't know a year ago—his likes, dislikes, passions, motivations, life dreams, idiosyncrasies, hobbies, sense of humor, and so on. I could tell you lots of things I admire about my friend, all because Beau has pulled back the curtains, allowing me a close-up glimpse into his life to see the real man. I *know* Beau.

You could say the same is true of God. We can know stuff about Him from observing what He has made—people, the earth and the heavens. The intricate design of humanity, the grandeur of our planet and the expanse of outer space all give us clues about the Creator. They communicate "big picture" things about Him. For example, through examining the human body, we know God possesses great *intelligence*. His blueprints for the eye and for DNA tell us He is *purposeful* (see Ps. 139:13-16). On a bigger scale, looking at what He has made on the earth tells us He is *creative*. Out of the same genius mind came the elephant and the eagle, the panther and the pelican, the ostrich and the otter, from creatures soaring above the earth to those crawling on it or swimming in the sea—God made them all (see Gen. 1:20-22). Or consider space, where some billions of galaxies like ours hang suspended in silence. This shows us "his eternal power and divine nature," which are "clearly seen from what has been made" (Rom. 1:20).

Knowledge about God is also within us. Like a hidden microchip, a basic understanding of right and wrong has been embedded within us by God. It's called conscience, and every person in every culture is born with one (see Rom. 2:14-15). Conscience is the thing that tells us we shouldn't murder or steal. I think God put it there to show us He is morally upright and *pure*.

Intelligence. Purpose. Creativity. Power. Purity.

If this was all we had, however, our knowledge of God would be incomplete. So He wrote a Book to give us a more detailed explanation about what He's like (a mystery we'll explore in chapter 7). But God didn't stop there. He decided to take this revelation thing to the ultimate level. This time He made it personal.

When God wanted to put a giant exclamation mark on His revelation to us, He sent His Son into the world. Jesus was God's ultimate *logo*, His last *Word* to us concerning Himself (see John 1:1-3).

No man has seen God at any time; the only begotten God who is in the bosom of the Father, He has *explained* Him (John 1:18, *NASB*, emphasis added).

Face it. The whole idea of "God" is sort of out there, isn't it? I mean, who can really put their arms round that concept? But Jesus explained God to us in a way that creation and Scripture can't (see John 1:14). Way beyond stars in the sky or words on a scroll, Jesus was the touchable God. He brush-stroked a detailed portrait of the invisible Deity (see Col. 1:15; 2:9). As the final piece of the God-puzzle, Jesus did more than speak our language. He actually *became* a man. Clothed in human skin, He showed us God through words, wonders and the way He treated people.

The Human-Friendly God

The mystery of the God-Man unfolds through what Jesus did. He was more than a walking billboard advertising the Father. He was more than a divine information machine, more than a prophet or a preacher. He was human in every way like us, and He experienced the same things we do—except He never did anything wrong (see John 1:14; Heb. 2:17).

He knows physical exhaustion and thirst and what it means to be hungry. He empathizes with weakness and suffering, even experiencing the weirdness of puberty and adolescence!

He understands emotions like anger, sadness, despair, stress, grief, disappointment and joy. He has ridden humanity's roller coaster.

Chapter 1

He faced common social adjustments, dealing with difficult people and experiencing social rejection.

He "grew in wisdom" and learning (Luke 2:52).

Whoa! Time out. How could Jesus grow in wisdom if He already possesses all knowledge? Well, you've just tapped into one of the deepest mysteries of the God-Man. It's not a mystery I can fully explain. Because Jesus was one of a kind, there's nothing in our experience to which we can compare Him. Though He was God, He somehow developed intellectually, learning like the rest of us.

Jesus also chose, as Man, to depend completely on the Father (another mystery). Through prayer and seeking the Father's will, Jesus matured and developed as a man in His relationship with God (see John 5:30; 8:49-50; 10:37).

Just like us.

A few years ago, I was watching my son Davis play T-League baseball. It was a typical summer Saturday afternoon at the ballpark, with parents in the stands sweating as much as the kids on the field. Seated behind the fence at home plate, I was talking with Ted, another dad whose boy was on my son's team. As Ted and I talked, our conversation was interrupted.

About ten yards away, we were distracted by three boys and their dad headed to the parking lot after their game. Because I also have three sons, I sympathized with his plight! But as the youngest of his three boys passed by, it was obvious that something was wrong. This little boy was walking with great difficulty, noticeably limping.

Observing more closely, Ted and I soon saw why. This little-leaguer, about six years old, had two artificial legs attached mid-

30

thigh. This tiny boy was hobbling along as fast as he could, determined to catch up with his older brothers. He was clearly having a lot of trouble, but they weren't about to wait on him (if you're the youngest child, you can identify with the insensitivity of older siblings!).

As his brothers ran on ahead to the car, the boy's dad patiently walked beside his youngest son, taking one step and then pausing to let his son catch up.

To my surprise, Ted suddenly called out, "Hey there, little fella."

Startled, the boy stopped, looking up from his concentration, his oversized baseball cap having fallen down over his ears.

"Come over here a second," Ted said, motioning with one hand.

Without hesitation, the tiny boy swiveled on his heels and began slowly hobbling over toward us. His dad paused, probably wondering what this strange man might want from his son. When the boy finally reached us, Ted spoke again.

"How are you doing today, buddy?" he asked.

"I'm okay, sir," the boy respectfully answered.

Ted then went on, "I noticed you've got some special legs there. How are they working out for you?"

The boy seemed surprised that someone would speak to him about his artificial limbs. Most people just stared at them or made fun of them. His dad also looked surprised and a bit concerned as Ted brought up what surely was a sensitive subject.

The boy glanced down at his legs and then looked back up at Ted, pushing his cap up so that he could see better. "Oh, they're okay, I guess," he replied.

"Well then, let me ask you something else. Do they ever rub a sore spot right here on your thighs?" Ted inquired, pointing to his own legs.

The boy's eyebrows raised up slightly. "Yes, sir, they sure do."

"And do you ever get cramps in your hips?" Ted asked.

This time the boy said nothing but slowly nodded his head up and down in agreement. *How could this man know these things about me?* he must have wondered to himself.

Ted smiled and said, "Well, I know exactly how you feel, buddy."

And then Ted did something I will never forget. Rolling up the cuffs of his jeans, he revealed two artificial legs of his own (which I later learned resulted from a car accident while in college). You can imagine my surprise at this revelation.

"Look here," Ted continued. "I've got some special legs just like you do."

The little boy's eyes suddenly brightened like the afternoon sun. It was obvious he had never known *anybody* who was just like him. You could see hope filling his six-year-old heart.

Ted sure saw it and added, demonstrating for the boy as he spoke, "You know what, little guy? When you adjust your straps like this, you can help make those bad old cramps go away. And if you put your weight right here on your legs, that'll keep those sore spots from hurting so much."

The boy's face lit up again with a huge smile. "Wow! Thanks, mister!"

"You're welcome," Ted said, chuckling to himself. "Now you better go catch up with your dad."

The boy hobbled his way back to his father, who was unsuccessfully holding back his tears. I detected a note of gratitude in the dad's eyes as he smiled at Ted and walked away. Meanwhile, I was choking back a baseball-sized lump in my throat, wiping away my own tears.

As the boy walked back to his dad that day, Ted simply turned and resumed watching our game as if nothing had happened.

By that point, however, baseball was the last thing on my mind. I had just watched a grown man hit a grand-slam homer in the life of a physically challenged kid. And while Ted nonchalantly crossed home plate and headed for the dugout, I sat motionless and speechless in the stands. I wondered, *What must it be like to miss your legs. What could it mean to meet someone else just like you who goes through life this way?*

Nobody understood what that little boy faced every day—what it meant to struggle out of bed, to make it to the breakfast table, to take a bath, or to hobble around the baseball field. Nobody knew what it felt like to be him—not his doctors, his physical therapists, his brothers, his best friend, even his parents.

Nobody except Ted.

Ted literally walked where that boy walked. He knew what he was going through, from the stigma to the struggles, from the embarrassment to the awkwardness—all the way down to the *exact spot* where it hurt.

Maybe you're like me, wondering at times if there are other people out there who understand what you're going through. Friends and family are a help because they love and care about you, but even they can't crawl inside and know what you're feeling in your most painful moments. Come to think of it, nobody can.

Nobody except Jesus.

As a man, Mary's Son felt every emotion and experience you do. Physically, intellectually, emotionally, socially and spiritually, He's been there. And beyond that, He's been in those places *for* you. He's felt what you've felt. He knows what it's like to walk on the artificial legs of your humanity. He knows what it's like to lose someone you love, to struggle with the awkwardness and ache that life brings. He knows the pain of separation, the emptiness of disappointment, the fear of abandonment, the wound of abuse, the stinging memory of hurtful words, the weariness of life. In short, He knows exactly what it's like to be *you*—all the way down to the *exact spot* where it hurts.

Jesus knows, and He cares.

Maybe you'll embrace that thought the next time you're sad, mad, glad, abandoned, lonely, depressed, abused, rejected, ridiculed, disappointed or deep in despair. Maybe you'll clothe yourself in the truth that there is One who calls out to you, motioning with His hand, calling you to come close, close enough to hear Him say, just like Ted, "Hey, I know how you feel."

* * *

The mystery of the God-Man is that He came to show us God and identify with our humanity. He was on a mission and was determined to complete the rescue operation. For Jesus, there would be no abort of the mission, no matter the obstacles or setbacks. Jesus intended to fulfill every part of the Father's brilliant plan for us (see John 3:17-18; 17:3-4).

The goal of that mission, and the hardest part, was to deliver us from our captivity to sin. The Son of God knew what sin had done to us. He had watched it from heaven. He had seen it up close for 33 years. But now He was about to experience it firsthand.

This meant the God-Man would have to suffer and suffer *big*. He would have to experience separation from God and the torment of His wrath (see Matt. 27:46; John 3:36; Rom. 6:23). I don't really get it, but try to imagine infinite anger and pain directed at you. *If* you can imagine such.

That's precisely what Jesus felt when He voluntarily laid down His life on the cross. During the crucifixion, God the Father unleashed unimaginable pain on the God-Man, the same pain that was waiting for you after death. Jesus felt the full sting of sin. Mysteriously, an eternity's worth of holy rage was compressed into six hours' time. This doesn't mean Jesus' physical sufferings were insignificant but only that the torture of sin fell on His total person—body *and* spirit. His pre-cross abuse was the appetizer for this torment, making Him so bloodied, bruised and beaten that He was hardly recognizable as a man (see Isa. 52:14). And He endured that for your hostage release.

Mysteriously, it was a brilliant plan gone wonderfully right.

CHAPTER 2

OF DEVILS AND DARKNESS

THE MYSTERY OF
EVIL AND SUFFERING

*Oh, the depth of the riches of the wisdom and
knowledge of God! How unsearchable his judgments,
and his paths beyond tracing out!*

Romans 11:33

Spontaneity—it's that rare ability to create life on a moment's notice. It's the antidote to boredom, the medicine that prevents monotony from slowly eating away at your life. Spontaneity can make you appear reckless, irresponsible and impulsive. But it can also make you look extremely impressive. It's an indispensable quality to have, especially when you're the father of three teenage boys. That's because adolescent boys require from their dads a certain level of random activity. Consequently, you must be prepared at any time to jump in the car, throw the football, play a video game, grab a burger, demonstrate a guitar chord, wrestle a wise guy, or rent an action movie. It's a tough job—sort of a cross between camp director and Navy Seal (my apologies to the Seals).

Friday evening following Thanksgiving, my wife and I had picked up our sons from a video game party at a local church and were on our way home when a random thought popped into my head.

"Hey, family . . . I've got a great idea. Let's go see a movie!"

"A movie?" my wife said. "It's 9:45. Is there a movie playing this late?"

"I hope so." I replied, "Besides, it's Thanksgiving weekend. C'mon. It'll be fun!"

Upon which a unified cheer rose from the back of the car.

That's what I'm talking about: spontaneity—random activity. I'm scoring major Dad points here. Stopping by our home to check online for movie times, I opened my laptop on the kitchen counter to discover that *National Treasure* was playing at a theater a few miles from our house. "Great movie!" I announced. "This is going to be an awesome night." As the movie was due to begin in 10 minutes, we raced out the door, arriving just in time for the previews.

By the time the movie ended, it was close to midnight. A misty rain had begun to fall, and it was getting quite cold—typical for a November night in Arkansas. Pulling into our driveway, we were still discussing the film. But as I opened the front door of our home, a strange feeling suddenly swept over me. It was an unexpected blast of cold air, as if I had mistakenly opened the door to a freezer. Confused as to where this cool breeze might be coming from, I proceeded cautiously into the entrance hall. Turning the corner, I discovered the source of the frigid air: The door leading down to our basement was wide open. That by itself wouldn't sufficiently explain the cold air unless . . . unless the exterior basement door was open.

You know that rush of adrenaline you get when something scary happens to you? I got that feeling.

"Clayton!" I said loudly. "Go upstairs and get my gun!"

Clayton leapt up the stairs in three strides, only to return seconds later and announce, "Dad, the guns are gone! All of them . . . and the ammo, too!"

Now you have to understand, as High Protector of the Kinleys, it's my sworn duty to keep the family safe at all times. So with an acute awareness of my fatherly responsibility, I ordered, "You guys stay here and I'll go around back and take a look."

Stealthily tiptoeing around the side of our house, I made my way to the backyard. Carefully peering around some lattice-work, I saw that our exterior basement door was gone. Oh, it wasn't just open or merely broken into. It was *gone*, ripped completely off its hinges, door casing and all! I leaned in farther, squinting my eyes for a better look. Now I'll confess, I can sometimes be a slow learner, and though the evidence was undeniable, it wasn't until that moment that I finally admitted the truth.

"We've been robbed!" I angrily said under my breath.

Just as I was about to enter the basement to check things out, something in my head said, *Jeff, don't!* So strong was that internal message, I almost looked over my shoulder to see if someone had just spoken to me. I'm convinced it was a warning from either God or a guardian angel.

At that moment, unbeknownst to me, my family, standing motionless and wild-eyed in the front hallway, heard the robbers slowly creeping down the back stairs leading to the basement . . . toward *me*! Had I proceeded through that doorway, I would have literally come face to face with them and a loaded gun. That voice may have saved my life! To paraphrase Shakespeare, discretion is the better part of valor—translated, *dumb bravery can get you killed.*

Hesitating after hearing the mysterious voice in my head, I raced back to the front of the house. On my arrival, my wife informed me that our uninvited guests were still in the house.

Armed with only a set of car keys and a torn movie stub, I knew I was no match for gun-wielding criminals. For all I knew, these guys were the kind that shoot you without a moment's hesitation, laughing at you while you bleed to death. That thought prompted me to issue a battle cry to my family.

"Outside! Now! Call 9-1-1!"

Now, if this had been a TV show, veteran law enforcement officials would have arrived within two minutes of the emergency call, tires screeching, lights flashing, sirens blaring, cars fish-tailing to a stop. But that's TV, not real life. Following six separate phone calls to 9-1-1 (the last three during which my wife used a few choice words), two uniformed officers finally arrived on the scene, almost 30 minutes after our first call for help. They searched the house with flashlights lit and guns drawn, but they found nothing.

As we filed the police report, we began noticing things that were missing: all our gaming equipment (Xboxes, iPods, PlayStations and games), DVD players and half our DVD collection, guns, ammunition and trigger locks. (I mentioned we have three teenage boys, right?)

But those possessions were small losses compared to what else was taken: two laptops—one being mine. Again, I can be slow to catch on, but it was at this point of realization that the robbery *really* hit me. I had placed my laptop on the kitchen counter to check out movie schedules and then left it there as we dashed out the door to the theater, as if I had purposely put it there in plain site so that the thieves would take it. I should have gift-wrapped it for them!

But the part that made me sick was that on that laptop was a manuscript that was due at my publisher's in two weeks! You'd think I had backed it up on a flash drive, right? Wrong.

It was gone. And there was no way on planet Earth that I could reproduce an entire manuscript from memory. Yet the game saver was that I had printed it out the week before, taking it with me to edit while away on a speaking engagement. Ultimately, we were able to scan it in and recover the book. And I met my deadline.

All in all, we lost about $6,000 worth of possessions—and our peace of mind, at least temporarily.

Although the boys and I reset the basement door before we went to bed, barricading it so well that an army of thieves could not get through, we hardly slept that night. Just knowing that thugs had invaded our home, stolen our stuff and made off into the night with bags of goodies made us wonder if they might come back for a return engagement. There were still more things to steal, right? After all, they had just struck pay dirt.

Over the next weeks and months, as we shored up our defenses (don't mess with the Kinleys now!) and wrangled with the police and the insurance company, we had many family discussions about evil and how to defend yourself against it.

And together we asked God, *Why?*

Stuff

I saw a bumper sticker the other day in my neighborhood. I see a lot of bumper stickers in my neighborhood. Some of them are funny. Some are philosophical. Some are rude. Some are sandwiched between 10 other stickers, competing for attention on the back of a faded '70s Volvo. One sticker I've seen says, *God wants spiritual fruit, not religious nuts.* Another reads, *Jesus loves you. Everyone else thinks you're an* [insert expletive here]. Another one says, *Hate is not a family value.* One reads, *Eve was framed.* And another, *God is a liberal.* (As you can see, I live in a very spiritual neighborhood.) Not to be outdone, I also have a sticker on my car. It says *The Beatles.*

My neighborhood has a lot of artists and activists—people who are creative and want to make a better world. They're also very diverse—morally, politically, philosophically and economically. But that's okay. We like different kinds of people. God told us He wanted us to live here and show them Jesus' love, so we're trying to do that.

Anyway, the other day in my neighborhood, I saw a bumper sticker that read, *Stuff happens*. (Well, it didn't exactly say "stuff," but you know what I'm talking about . . . *stuff*.)

It's an interesting philosophy to consider: *Stuff happens*. All kinds of stuff. Bad stuff. Good stuff. Painful stuff. Inconvenient stuff. Stuff that affects your view of life. Stuff that messes with your mind. Stuff that screws up your emotions. Random stuff. Big stuff. Little stuff. Global stuff. Personal stuff. Stuff that makes you throw your hands up in the air and cry out, "Oh, no! I don't believe it. Not again. Why me?"

But the real mystery is *why* stuff happens. Bombings. Terrorist attacks. School shootings. Murder. Rape. Plane crashes. Car wrecks. Sickness. Disease. Natural disasters. Divorce. And of course, *robbery*. From flat tires to F-4 tornados. From people stealing your place in line at the grocery store to your boss stealing your retirement through a corporate scandal. It's everything from life's minor annoyances to unmistakable acts of evil. You know what I'm talking about, don't you?

Stuff.

Evil stuff.

Evil is a mystery as old as mankind. For centuries, it has given birth to lots of pain and suffering. I once heard a philosopher refer to it as "inconvenient life occurrences." Let me tell you about one such occurrence.

My friend Chris works at our neighborhood coffee shop. I like Chris. He's a cool guy. Until recently, he had a beard. He's a musician who owns bagpipes. I like having a friend who owns bagpipes. It makes me want to wear a kilt and quote lines from *Braveheart*. Chris also plays a djembe, which is a kind of hand drum. Or he did until about a year ago. Sitting in his living room one night, some people kicked in his door, tied him up, put him in a closet and started stealing his things. Chris tried to escape, and they shot at him. The bullet went through the tendon between his thumb and index finger. Now Chris has trouble playing his djembe. You could call what Chris experienced an inconvenient life occurrence, or you could call it karma or bad luck or anything you like. Chris calls it *stuff*.

Some people who believe in God call it evil. (Maybe somebody should make a new bumper sticker that says, *Evil happens.*)

Of course, we can understand reasons why some suffering occurs. If you hit your boss over the head with your computer monitor, you'll suffer through a few months in jail (and the hassle of being unemployed). If you decide to speed through a red light, you may end up totaling your car or your face. Suffering because of a selfish act or poor decision is easy to understand. That's a no-brainer. But it gets a little more complicated when you ask, Why do innocent people suffer? Why do those who didn't do anything wrong still suffer tragedy? Why does evil visit *them*?

Earthquakes, terrorist attacks, tsunamis, child abductions, murders, car accidents and cancer, birth defects and identity theft—you can intellectually dismiss some of these by blaming shifts in the Earth's crust or by pointing out that the world contains greedy people who occasionally commit criminal acts.

But that still doesn't answer the deeper questions: Why doesn't God prevent these things from occurring? Why doesn't He stop bad stuff from happening to good folks? I can understand why an evil man has a piano fall on his head: He simply got what was coming to him. But the real mystery is why God stands silently on the sidelines and watches while buildings fall on good people . . . people He claims to love!

Would you just stand by and watch someone brutally torture and kill your best friend, husband, wife, son or daughter? Of course you wouldn't. Yet the One who created mankind in His own image—the One who calls us His children and His bride, the One who says He loves us with an infinite, everlasting love—allows all this stuff to happen.

Why?

You can't blame the tumor that took your mother or the bullet that robbed you of your brother. You can't point a finger at the wind that destroyed your home. Yet we feel like we have to blame something or some*one*. It's basic cause and effect here. Someone is ultimately responsible; otherwise, the universe is out of control and chaos rules.

Harold S. Kushner, in his book *When Bad Things Happen to Good People*, writes that most of life (and the universe) is orderly, but there are "pockets of chaos" that dot our lives. That's one way to look at it. But you could equally argue the opposite: Much of life is actually random and chaotic, occasionally punctuated with sporadic episodes of order.

Why?

Some religious people will correct you here, saying you're not supposed to ask why. "It's not right to question the Lord," they say. But maybe it's not an issue of being *right* as much as it is an issue of simply being *real*. Asking questions about why bad stuff happens doesn't mean you're not godly. It just means you are a thinking human being. God's not insecure. He can surely handle our tough questions, right? And this one is the mother of all toughies.

In His Word, God never hides the fact that stuff happens; in fact, He made sure a lot of it got put in the Bible. My mind races to the Old Testament where God says He'll curse Israel if they disobey Him (see Deut. 11:26-28). (They did a lot of cursing in the Old Testament. Not cussing . . . *cursing*. They still do that today in the Middle East. In modern-day Iraq, one man can insult another by proclaiming, "Curses upon your mustache!" I've never had my mustache cursed, but I imagine it's a pretty traumatic experience. Maybe it causes your hair to grow up instead of down.)

Some people today think God is still in the cursing business. They think that most (if not every) evil or bad event—from the World Trade Center attack to a malignant tumor to a runny nose—is somehow God's way of punishing us for something wrong we've done. You may recall that after 9/11, a few self-proclaimed "prophets" claimed God was punishing our country for a host of evils, from allowing abortion to removing prayer from schools. These people view God as a celestial traffic cop, lying in wait to pounce on us whenever we commit some explicit or secret sin. But if that were the case, we're all pretty much busted, right? Game over. However, since we're not all suffering torment and calamity 24-7, there must be some other explanation for why bad stuff happens (or doesn't happen).

The way I see it, God has to be in control or else He's not God. And though He does discipline His children when they sin, He's not out to destroy our lives. According to Jesus, that's Satan's job (see John 10:10). And it's clear from the Bible that punishment isn't God's motivation behind every bad thing that happens. Saying evil is God's way of punishing us may be the easiest way to make sense of things that don't make sense in the world.

But I don't buy it.

The Good with the Bad

There's a story in the Bible of this guy named Job. Do you remember him? He hung out about 5,000 years ago, about the time of Abraham. According to the Bible, Job was a great man with a terrific family. Wealthy, too. Loaded with real estate and cattle. Job was the total package—rich and righteous.

Now, for some mysterious reason, God gave Satan permission to go postal on him—destroying his fortune, killing most of his family and robbing him of his health. Now that's a bad day! (You may recall that many years later Satan asked permission to attack Peter like this [see Luke 22:31]—Jesus never said whether or not permission was given.) Job's children were taken from him and his body festered up with these huge boils that constantly oozed. The only thing that Job had left was a nagging wife who encouraged him to "curse God and die!" (Job 2:9). Nice wife, huh?

Job's story illustrates the worst kind of life disaster. That's the kind of *stuff* I'm talking about.

The Bible never indicates that any of this happened as punishment for Job. Rather, it came as a result of a conversation between God and the devil about whether or not Job would curse God. Of course, some people doubt this conversation actually took place because they question the literal existence of a creature called Lucifer. They believe he's a figure conjured up, a convenient imaginary villain invented to personify our inconvenient behavior.

For these people, he's not lurking in the shadows, secretly plotting his next sinister attack against humanity in general or *you* specifically. There are no minions of Satan, no dark spirits with sulphuric breath, perched and prepared to swoop down into our lives, causing trouble, disaster and calamity.

I choose to believe they're very real and that Satan did talk to God about Job.

This conversation between God and the devil seems a bit odd to me, though, because it almost reads like some sort of bet, like God and Satan are playing deep-space poker, using people as chips. Of course, if we believe God is loving and personal, we would reject that idea—and rightly so. But then how do we understand this deal between God and the devil? If that's the way things work up in heaven, then does God still make those kinds of deals today? Has Satan ever approached the Lord to discuss me? Or you?

Anyway, following all manner of evil descending on Job's head, he understandably had a lot of questions for God—sadly, he didn't get too many answers. In the end, however, Job did prosper, becoming richer than he had been before. He had more children and he regained his health.

The fact remains that both good and bad, both curses and blessings, appear to randomly fall on people, regardless of their religious preferences or lifestyle. So how do we explain that? We can look at this problem several ways:

1. *Evil happens because God's not really there after all.* That would certainly explain why He does nothing!

2. *God's there, but He doesn't care what happens to us.* Of course, that raises even more questions like, What about all those verses that say He cares? Does this mean the Bible isn't true?

3. *God's there and He cares, but He can't do anything about evil because He's not powerful enough.* This would mean that His enemy (Satan) is an equally strong and worthy opponent and often gets the better of God by foiling His plans for mankind. That would explain why sometimes good things happen and sometimes bad things happen. It's like an ongoing rivalry between two college football teams—on any given day, you never know who'll win. So who's leading the series here? Who has more wins?

4. *God really does care, but because of all the sin in our lives, He has to punish us regularly to remind us of how bad we are and to keep us in line.* So evil and suffering are like painful reminders of our badness and our need

to be holy—kind of like finding a gray hair is just one more reminder you're getting older.

5. *God doesn't dislike us; He's just unconcerned.* You know—He's detached, aloof, like an absent father. That's the idea here: God is too distracted to even think of us much at all.

6. *God, as Creator of all things, is somehow also the author of the evil.* After all, He is in charge, isn't He?

This topic is definitely not the warm fuzzy part of our faith. In fact, this mystery of evil gives me indigestion. (Thinking deeply sometimes does that to me.) And here's another deep dilemma: If God knew Adam and Eve's original disobedience would lead to all the evil and suffering we see in our world today, why then did He allow it in the first place? Didn't He know that if He gave Lucifer freedom to choose and rebel, Lucifer would end up deceiving humanity? Didn't He know that in order to repair us, Christ would have to suffer unimaginable punishment for our sins? Wasn't He aware that Eve would cave in to temptation and that the rest of humanity would be ruined? Didn't He understand all the polluting effects of sin—disease, hate, evil—that would end up downstream?

Of course He did.

But He still let it happen. And He hasn't stopped it yet. That river of sin still flows through history, making life ugly and painful for anyone—make that *everyone*—in its path. You can get angry, frustrated or bitter. But at whom? God? Humankind?

Society? Your parents? Your neighbor? Yourself? The devil? Mother Nature? All of the above?

And do you think things will ever get better? Or are we merely pawns in some galactic chess match of good versus evil? Are *we* the battlefield of gods? Is there such a thing as pure evil, or is there just relative degrees of goodness? Can we ever make any sense out of this mystery?

Tough questions. And just when we think we have it figured out, life throws us a curve ball and knocks our theological equation out of the batter's box. So where do we go for answers? Is there anything that will shed even a single ray of light on this age-old mystery?

Sadistic Parenting

Could there be some unknown, unseen reason why God allows bad stuff to happen to us? Could He be orchestrating some grander scheme, something that intersects so far above our heads that to explain it to us would be like trying to communicate nano-technology to a donkey—or to me?

Mark and I have been friends for years. He's a great guy with an infectious (and often sick) sense of humor. He's also the only guy I know who knows more about the Beatles than I do. Mark's son is tight with my three sons. He and Debi are also parents to three beautiful daughters. One of those girls was born on the same day as my oldest son, on the same hospital floor, just a few feet and a few hours apart. (I think this means they're supposed to get married.) Several years ago, my wife and I accepted the honor of becoming godparents to Mark and Debi's kids. (I like the idea of being called *the Godfather*.)

Anyway, some years back Mark did something that appeared to be very out of character for a good dad like him. When his daughter Ashley was about three, he hired a team of people to forcibly hold her down while a strange man crammed needles into her precious little head. Screaming in excruciating pain and confusion, Ashley wondered why the man she had grown to love and trust stood by and watched while his daughter was tortured in this way. Imagine the look in her innocent young eyes. Can you envision the pain and suffering she went through? And all the while calling out for Daddy to help. But Daddy simply stood there, doing nothing.

Lest you think my friend Mark is some sort of sadistic creature, let me use the wide-angle lens on that situation—that might help you go a little easier on him. Earlier that day while playing, Ashley had fallen and split open her scalp. With blood gushing from her pretty little head, Mark rushed her to the emergency room. The ER team had to work quickly to stop the bleeding and close the wound. Because most young girls in pain don't sit motionless while needles are being dug into their scalp, the nurses had to physically restrain Ashley while the doctor meticulously sewed up her head. And Mark stood there, with full authority and power to stop the painful procedure at any time . . . but he didn't! On the contrary, he wanted it to happen. Yet he also hurt through the process.

Unknown to Ashley at the time, allowing this inconvenient evil was necessary to bring about something better. It wasn't until years later that Mark's actions made sense to his daughter. At the time, it simply didn't add up for her. Ashley had zero ability to understand that the strategy for her ultimate healing included some temporary pain and discomfort. Had Mark stuck his face into the middle of Ashley's ER surgery and explained all this to her, she still probably wouldn't have understood. All she really knew was (1) I'm suffering, and (2) Dad is doing nothing about it.

Isn't that how we feel sometimes?

Now I'm not suggesting a direct parallel between this story and how God treats us, and I'm not suggesting that we suffer because it's good for us or because there's some secret lesson we must learn. All I am saying is that when our Father seems to be callously standing by, He is nevertheless still there—and in charge of the situation. And He alone knows how this evil fits into the bigger picture.

Evil is like one stroke of an artist's brush that seems out of character with the rest of the painting, but when you step back and take in the big picture, you can better appreciate its purpose. Or consider a symphony or band. Plug in your earphones and try to pick out one instrument (like a flute or bass guitar) and track its part through the song. By itself, it doesn't sound like much, and may even sound unattractive or out of character with the rest of the piece. But then allow your ears to step back and listen to the whole symphony or group. Suddenly that one instrument makes more sense and is more palatable to the ears. It's like reading the lyrics to a song but never hearing the music: The words are a part of the story, not the whole story.

I think our suffering and the evil that happens in life are like that—a dissonant chord in an otherwise harmonious melody. Considering the bigger picture of life at least lets us know that our suffering isn't all there is and that it won't last forever.

I'm convinced there are no easy answers here. There isn't always a satisfactory explanation to the whys of life. And to be honest, some answers may never come in this lifetime. So that leaves us with some options:

1. We can become bitter and angry.
2. We can try to ignore the bad stuff.
3. We can grow numb and become depressed.
4. We can choose to trust in a God whose ways we do not always understand.

The first option will make you old and unhappy, but it's the most natural one. The second response will make you an existentialist, robbing you of any chance to enjoy life. The third option is easy but will turn you into an emotional zombie. The last option is the most illogical choice and, when you think about it, the hardest. The most difficult thing to do is to trust that an unseen Father is watching you, caring for you, controlling events around you even when your world is falling apart. In reality, faith in God isn't always logical; it doesn't always make sense or seem like a good idea.

When I think back on our Thanksgiving-weekend heist and wonder about the evil that befell us, I am forced to ask, *Why did this happen? What are we supposed to learn from this experience?* Maybe if there were any lessons to learn, it would be to back up my computer files. Of course, I also learned why all my neighbors had alarm systems. I was thankful no one was hurt and that we hadn't come home five minutes earlier. But what never crossed my mind was that there was some unknown sin we had committed to deserve this. I believe evil happened that night because some people have no respect for their fellow humans. The evil in those thieves prompted them to take what wasn't theirs. And I found myself wishing great curses and calamity on their heinous hooded heads. And on their mustaches.

An Inside Job

Honestly, I hate evil. I hate what it has done to my world, to the environment, to my country, my city, my neighborhood and my fellow humans. I hate what it has done to people I know—how it has wrecked marriages, destroyed families and scarred children. But more than that, I hate what evil has done to *me*. It's one thing to recognize the wickedness of the devil—and we can't overestimate his capabilities—but it's not the devil that scares me. I can overcome him (see 1 John 4:4). In spite of what he would want me to believe, he's not my biggest problem. No, the evil that most affects me is *in* me. What haunts my life is that vestige of sinfulness left over from Adam's foray in the Garden. This infectious virus is within me, *heir*borne—spread from parent to child, passed down from generation to generation. There is disease in our DNA, friend.

And that is also a mystery.

It's the liar, the murderer and the terrorist living in my heart that makes me want to call 9-1-1. Why evil still loiters in my soul is a conundrum that confuses me every day. It's the worst kind of thief, the one that most often robs me of life's best. It's the part of me that secretly enjoys seeing my enemy fail, the part of me that loves to hate, the part that lusts, the part that refuses to believe, the part that enjoys doing what makes God cry.

You can take the idea of evil and translate it into a principle that rules the world or you can see it as a satanic persona. Both are very true and real. But until you realize that the evil native to the human heart is the biggest threat to your personal homeland security, you will never scratch the surface of the real problem. Dealing with the devil within, that dark part of you, may not prevent tragedy in the world, but it can have a huge effect on those with whom you live, work and play. And it can make a huge difference in *your* life.

You might expect at this point in the story that I might offer three steps for dealing with your sinful nature. I won't. But I will say this: We'd be a lot better off if more people—more Christian people—would stop pointing condemning fingers at the world around them and launch a holy crusade within. I have to look at me first before I can look at you. I have to own up to my own selfish thoughts, attitudes and behavior. Then, and only then, can I deal with the bigger problem of evil in the world.

The real mystery is me.

The real mystery is you.

And the only solution is a daily change of heart.

* * *

God's role in evil and suffering is a big mystery. No doubt about that. His relationship to the devil is pretty sketchy too (or at least confusing). So what do we know for sure? We know God sometimes causes suffering. We know He lets bad stuff happen. That's an inconvenient truth, and there's no getting around it. We know that Satan is a lion with an insatiable appetite for humans and that he's on a very long leash (see 1 Pet. 5:8). We also know that one day all his activities *will* cease and that he'll get his (see Rev. 20:10).

I'm certain that some evil and suffering are caused by humans. Other tragedies are brought on by a creation (including our planet) that is deteriorating. Some bad stuff is caused by the devil, but not without God's permission. Christ's followers have been called to wage war in the conflict of good versus evil—fighting injustice, abuse and inequality, bringing the hope of Jesus to a hurting and sinful world. Maybe less evil would happen if we all lived what we say we believe. Maybe more good stuff would happen if we loved our neighbors, especially the ones that make us want to cuss (and curse).

Job learned that there is a time to plead your case before God and a time to quietly sit and think about the fact that He is God and you're not.

We do know that God will eventually triumph over evil. *That* is not a mystery. But until then, you and I walk this tightrope stretched precariously between faith and fate. And we choose to trust—even when all we have is a Father's promise—or we cave in to despair.

Either way, we live with tension—and mystery.

CHAPTER 3

THE READING OF THE WILL

THE MYSTERY OF PREDESTINATION

Before I formed you in the womb I knew you.

Jeremiah 1:5

It's a frigid fall Friday night at Morgan Manor. A palatial estate nestled in the Catskill Mountains of upstate New York, the manor is a well-known fixture in the area. Equally wealthy neighbors make up what is popularly referred to as blueblood country, home to the haves and the envy of the have-nots. You don't *move into* this part of the upstate; you are *born* into it.

A biting northern wind cuts through the huge 100-year-old trees lining the half-mile drive leading up to the main house. Their burnt-orange leaves, once green with life, are whipped up and scattered across the lawn of the grand estate, a visual reminder that all things must pass. In the reality of life, leaves change color and then fall, letting go of their life source and cascading downward to be eventually absorbed into the earth. It's a "dust to dust" kind of thing. And what is true for leaves is also true for humans.

Inside the estate, the Morgan family gathers in the wood-paneled library for a somber occasion—the reading of Jacob Morgan's will. Flames dance softly in the fireplace. Hardly a sound is heard above the crackling of burning maple wood. Everyone necessary is present, including Morgan's widow, noticeably younger than the aged billionaire tycoon. A late-in-life addition to Morgan's "trophy case" of acquisitions, Judith was formerly an employee at Morgan's equestrian farm. The rumor mill circulated the story that Morgan had simply divorced his former wife to trade her in for a newer model. Now in her 50s and hardened by the pretense and façade of life at the top of the food chain, Judith has endured countless cocktail parties and a near addiction to plastic surgery. She barely resembles the 27-year-old, free-spirited horse lover she once was.

Beside her sits Morgan's defiant stepdaughter and estranged son—both grown with children of their own. Even Morgan's freeloading nephew is there. Sam Morgan bears no resemblance to his deceased 80-year-old uncle and shared nothing in common with him other than the same last name and a love for gambling. What wealth his own father had left to him has long since been squandered in a string of bad business deals and shady investments. Having driven up from Jersey, Sam was hoping for one last morsel to drop from the Morgan table.

Emotionally on edge and pretending not to care, they all eagerly await the official reading. No one dares make eye contact with one another as the executor enters the room and takes his seat behind Jacob Morgan's commanding oak desk. Carefully placing his reading glasses on the tip of his nose, he clears his throat and begins reading the last will and testament.

It all comes down to this. Months of legal maneuvering and social jockeying have inspired great expectations. Hollow hopes and empty wishes mean little at this point. Assurances made by the family patriarch while he was alive carry little weight now. Past promises have expired. Earlier verbal nods are null and void. This night is all that matters now. This document is the only real deal—what is written and read here will become law.

Tonight, mystery will give birth to reality. Hope will give birth to either happiness or heartache. The reading of this document will reveal what was really on the heart and mind of dear old Jacob before his passing. This is his will—his ultimate and final desire—and like it or not, everyone will have to live with it. But along with revealing who gets the Ferrari, the beach house and a sizeable share of stock in the company, Jacob Morgan may just have a few postmortem surprises up his sleeve for those he has preceded in death. A harsh and controlling man while alive, Morgan always had to have the final word in all conversations and negotiations.

Tonight will be no different.

A last will and testament reveals a lot about a person. It tears away at façade and pretense, stripping away false expectations. It tells you more about the individual than perhaps you really want to know. It X-rays the heart of the deceased, exposing the deepest loves and desires of the one whose name is indelibly signed in ink at the bottom of the document.

A Will of a Different Sort

For obvious reasons, God doesn't have a last will and testament. And He's certainly not some cold, cranky old codger who's out for revenge. But He has expressed His ultimate desires, originally decreed in eternity past and written down in time for us. It's His will, but it's not what you might think. It's not some elusive religious road map or some puzzle game to figure out. It's not a call to resign yourself to some immovable force resembling something just this side of blind fate (as in "I guess it was just God's will"). And it's not about seven steps to finding God's mate for your life or choosing the right career.

What we're talking about here is more about exploring what was really on the Almighty's mind back in eternity, before time began. It's about what was written in His heart. His original desire. His innermost intentions. The choices He has purposed deep within Himself. What pleases Him. His will. And unlike the will of a human—God's will cannot be contested or changed. It simply is what it is. But what is it?

It's a mystery found lurking in the shadows of an enigma known as *predestination*, the proposition that God planned our eternal destiny "before the creation of the world" (Eph. 1:4). The word itself sounds rather clinical, doesn't it? Cold and impersonal? Unfriendly? It's a subject so controversial that it causes some people to immediately recoil in angry rejection at its mere suggestion. And at the heart of the controversy is this: Did God choose some people for salvation while purposefully ignoring others before they had a chance to choose or reject Him? And if so, why would He do something like that? Does this mean our fate is sealed before we're even born? Can we be anything other than fleshy robots, puppets whose strings are pulled by an unseen puppeteer? If not, how could a fair and just God do something like this? Or is it somehow possible that God found a way for our will to mysteriously and perfectly harmonize with His own?

Heavy stuff, right?

Predestination is the stuff that plays with your head. It messes with your mind because of its profound implications regarding who God is and who *we* are. If predestination is really true and it means what it sounds like it means, then we may find our entire view of God shockingly re-imagined. It may also radically alter the image that stares back at us in the mirror.

Rock of Ages

One of the coolest places on the planet is the British Museum. Mummies, ancient relics from extinct civilizations, coins, medals, drawings, city gates from Assyria, famous sculptures from ancient Rome and Greece—they're all there, and much more. You could spend days gazing in awe at the thousands of historical artifacts housed in that massive facility. It's arguably the most extensive collection of historical and prehistorical artifacts assembled anywhere in the world.

Not so long ago, I was browsing the museum's exhibits when I came face to face with one of the most amazing archaeological discoveries and the museum's most famous attraction. This exhibit draws a consistently larger crowd than all the others. It's a 3-foot-9-inch by 2-foot-4-inch piece of granite 11 inches thick and weighing about three-quarters of a ton, and it's been on exhibit at the museum since 1802. What's the big deal about this big slab of rock?

Discovered in 1799 by soldiers in Napoleon's army, this rock, the Rosetta Stone (so named because of where it was found), contains an Egyptian hieroglyphic text that up until that time was undecipherable. Fortunately, the stone's hieroglyphics are also accompanied by a Greek translation, which meant that for the first time in modern history, hieroglyphics could be decoded, opening a huge window of unparalleled insight and understanding into ancient Egypt. It's one of the greatest treasures of human history—right up there with the Dead Sea Scrolls and King Tut's tomb.

If there is any truth to the mystery of predestination, then it becomes a Rosetta Stone of sorts, translating a deeper insight and understanding into God, humanity and life—even opening a window into eternity itself. But can this mystery be decoded? Let's start with what we know.

According to Scripture, God is a *choosing* God. But we would expect as much, seeing as how He possesses mind, emotion and will. Anybody with a will can choose, right? You and I can choose, so why can't God?

In fact, the Bible claims that God chose individuals for salvation and that His choice of them was totally unrelated to their behavior (see John 15:16; Eph. 1:11; 1 Thess. 1:4). In other words, they did nothing to cause God to choose them.

> From the beginning God chose you to be saved through the sanctifying work of the Spirit and through belief in the truth (2 Thess. 2:13).

Now, if that statement doesn't disturb you, you're probably not getting it yet. Read it again. If it does bother you, you're pretty normal.

But here's where the mystery takes a twist and gets a little hairy. According to that same Bible, it's equally clear that you also have a say-so in the matter of your destiny.

> But if serving the LORD seems undesirable to you, then *choose for yourselves* this day whom you will serve, whether the gods your forefathers served beyond the River, or the gods of the Amorites, in whose land you are living. But as for me and my household, we will serve the LORD (Josh. 24:15, emphasis added).

> They hated knowledge and *did not choose to fear the LORD* (Prov. 1:29, emphasis added).

Believe in the Lord Jesus, and you will be saved—you and
your household (Acts 16:31, emphasis added; see also
Mark 16:16; Acts 2:21; Rom. 10:9,13).

We get to choose, too. Confused yet?

Here are the obvious questions: How is it possible for God
to genuinely choose individuals *before* time, and those same
individuals choose Him *in* time? How can both choices be genuine, authentic and free? And if He chooses this for us, what
else has He already planned for us?

Of course, we could just stop right here, toss out the whole
idea of predestination and be on our merry way. Just skip this
chapter and move on to the next mystery, right? I mean, to begin
with, predestination sounds so unfair. How do you account for
all the people who have never heard of Jesus? Don't they get a
chance, too? And what about the mentally challenged? What
about the millions of innocent babies whose lives have been cut
short by a woman's choice? They never even had a chance to be
bad or good or make a choice. God's supposed to be fair and
give everyone a chance, right? Isn't that part of what makes Him
a just and good God? Can He still be God and do that? And
doesn't the Bible say anyone can go to heaven who wants to (see
John 6:40; Acts 2:21)? Besides, the idea of predestination appears
to completely contradict our basic understanding of God and
Jesus. Predestination makes God sound like He doesn't love
everyone. But the Bible says He loves the whole world and that
Jesus died for everyone (see John 3:16; 1 John 2:2).

Part of what complicates this mystery is that the word "predestined" is actually in the Bible (see Rom. 8:29-30; Eph. 1:5,11).

And any way you slice it—from the original Greek word to the context of the verses where it's found—the word "predestine" always means to "predetermine, or decide beforehand"—*always*. That's a hard one for me to ignore, assuming the Bible always tells the truth. And consider that all the times the Bible says God chooses—whether the choice is a nation or an individual—that choice is never based on who the person is or what he or she has done. In other words, God's choice of them is never earned or caused by the good deeds of the one chosen.

Now, you *could* try to redefine the word and make it say something less offensive. You could just say, "It isn't true and it doesn't mean what you think it means." Many people—theologians and entire denominations included—have done this and seem to be quite content with their conclusions. And it doesn't seem to bother them or affect the way they relate to God. They appear to be fairly comfortable with their belief. And they are fruitful Christians.

But doing this just may create more confusion than insight. As we saw in the last chapter, trying to perfectly reconcile God and reality often brings more tension than illumination. The truth is, we can't run from, redefine or brush off the hard stuff about God just because it's inconvenient or prickly.

Mystery lovers have to dig deeper.

Obviously, we won't fully crack this case or get our minds completely around the subject in one chapter, but we can still dust for fingerprints and see what we can uncover. By beginning with what is apparently clear, we can work our way back and hopefully navigate through the fog of this mystery without running into a brick wall.

To me, it breaks down like this: Assuming that God really did choose somebody like you for salvation, what was His motivation? Why did He do it? Here are some of the possibilities:

1. *God randomly chose you.* You got lucky. A few people win the lottery, but most don't—and the same thing happened here. God randomly chose you as if He were picking the winning lottery numbers. He did it this way because He's God and He can do whatever He wants. Case closed. Now just move on and enjoy your winnings.

2. *God has favorites.* God fast-forwarded time, pressed *play* when He got to you and saw something that He liked. He chose you because you helped a stranded motorist once or because you let smelly old Aunt Gert hug you at that family reunion. The bottom line? You did something right and got yourself chosen. It's as simple as that.

3. *God made salvation available through Jesus and then sat back and hoped real hard you'd choose Him.* So in other words, God put salvation on the buffet of life, then stepped behind the counter and politely asked, "Can I help you?" In this scenario, all the pressure is on the one choosing. God is merely the celestial salesman hoping you'll buy His product.

4. *God's only way to save you was to choose you.* He had no other options available to Himself. Because (along

with the rest of humankind) you're officially dead in sin and unable to take a positive step toward God (see Rom. 3:10-12; Eph. 2:1), He predestined you to make that choice. God (by necessity) was the initiator, taking the first step in the relationship.

5. *God just wanted to do it.* He had the option to let you go your way and pass into eternity and judgment, but instead, He chose you, even though He didn't have to. There was no law or force that obligated the Creator to select you for salvation. No one twisted His arm until He cried *uncle.* He did it simply because He wanted to. Because He loved you. Because it pleased Him to redeem and cleanse a corrupt heart like yours. Because in the grand scheme of things, it's all about God and His glory. He knew that choosing you would bring Him praise—now and in eternity. So out of love and a compulsion to honor His own gracious character, He simply did it.

According to the Bible, you might confidently eliminate the first three of these possibilities (see Eph. 2:8-9). But what about the others?

The Death of Santa Claus

Sitting in the college cafeteria as a freshman, I had just finished another gourmet meal the cooks entitled "Taco Surprise" (the surprise came about an hour later). A few of us students were huddled around a table talking to one of the most respected professors on campus. He was the kind of prof who enjoyed spending time with lowly underclassmen like us, shooting the breeze over a cup of coffee—the kind of guy whose office door was always open. For some reason in the course of our conversation that day, the topic of predestination came up, and I immediately objected to the idea.

"God can't do that," I protested. "It wouldn't be fair."

I don't remember there being a lengthy discussion or anyone getting upset. But I do recall Dr. Meredith's simple challenge to me: "Jeff, when you get back to your room, why don't you read Ephesians chapter one . . . slowly."

"I'll do that," I replied confidently.

Trotting across campus, I arrived back at my dorm room, grabbed my pocket New Testament from my backpack, dove onto my bed and dug into the first few verses of Ephesians. That's when I read these words:

> For he chose us in him before the creation of the world to be holy and blameless in his sight. In love he predestined us to be adopted as his sons through Jesus Christ, in accordance with his pleasure and will—to the praise of his glorious grace, which he has freely given us in the One he loves (Eph. 1:4-6).

To be honest, my first response when I read those verses was a wave of emotion (and it wasn't the Taco Surprise kicking in). I reread those verses, and once more I felt the same sensation. It was the same exact feeling I had had as a child when I accidentally discovered a brand-new bicycle in my parents' bedroom on Christmas Eve. It was then the reality hit me—and hit me hard—almost catapulting me out of my footy-pajamas: *There is no Santa Claus.*

With the simple opening of a door, my lifelong illusion about Christmas instantly shattered, and my mental images and emotions associated with December 25 forever changed. In a heartbeat, my perspective was never the same. Of course, I got over it. But through that unintentional discovery, I experienced something I had never known before.

From that day forward, I understood that Santa Claus wasn't rewarding me each year because I had been good. He hadn't seen me when I was sleeping or known when I was awake. In reality, all those presents of every past Christmas— the G.I. Joes, the slot car racing set, the microscope, the guitar and amplifier—were the gracious gifts of loving parents who wanted the very best for me and who had sacrificed dearly to make sure I opened good presents on Christmas morning. I had been living in a fantasy world all those years—a world created by society and perpetuated by my parents and my overactive imagination.

Not that I regretted believing in St. Nick all those years. As most children do, I enjoyed the rush of expectation that filled me during the Christmas season. Those are some of my greatest childhood memories. It's just that through opening my parents' door that night, my eyes were opened to something *better* than Santa Claus. The magic of my make-believe world melted into reality. I now had someone to thank for all those gifts. Someone I could love every day of the year, not some fat man with smelly breath whose lap I sat on one day a year.

Fast-forward 10 years. Lying on that college dorm bed, I once again felt a door opening. And through it, I saw something I had never seen before, though it was there all along. Similar to my Christmas Eve enlightenment, I was shocked. Even somewhat numbed. Then my shock subsided, turning to mild disillusionment. I asked myself, *How could such a thing be true? How could God* choose? *How could God choose* me? But the more I opened my heart and mind, my disillusion turned to wonder, which soon became amazement. For the first time in my life, I understood what "Amazing Grace" meant.

And that's when I started to worship.

I began imagining what this truth said about God, about who He really is and how He operates. If God chooses, how does this affect the way He interacts with history, mankind, nations and individuals? If God chooses, what other things had He predetermined? (For example, see Acts 2:23.) I felt as if I had stumbled on a secret room in God's house, one that had been there all along, but one I had never entered before. I had never even turned the doorknob and peeked in. It was a room that opened up a world of discovery and understanding. And it also led to a world of unanswered questions.

I asked myself, *If the only way I can be saved is for God to first choose me, then what does that say about* me? *Could I be worse off than I had originally thought? More ruined? More broken? Was I really dead in sin,* unable *to choose God on my own?*

But it also confounded me that the Bible clearly says I chose God, too. That was undeniable and just as true as God's choice of me. My mind continued manufacturing question marks when I realized that "all people everywhere" are called, even required, "to repent" (Acts 17:30). But how can God require all people to repent when He apparently hasn't chosen everyone for salvation?

I don't know.

How can He be a just God and yet not give people a genuine chance to do what He requires them to do?

I don't know.

How can He choose some but not all?

I don't know.

I suspect the answer lies somewhere on the map between the village of my limited understanding and the world of God's sovereignty. In which case I must be the village idiot. There's a verse that says, "As the heavens are higher than the earth, so are my ways higher than your ways and my thoughts than your thoughts" (Isa. 55:9). And just how high are the heavens above the earth? Six miles? One hundred miles? One hundred million miles? A hundred billion light-years? Or maybe just too high to bother measuring.

I suspect this whole predestination thing qualifies to head the mystery category. I mean, we're in way over our heads here. The waves are too big and the undertow too strong. Maybe you're the kind of person who is content to stand on the shore and marvel at the majesty of the ocean. With the sea mist spraying your face, you're strangely comforted by the sound of powerful waves crashing against the shore. Or perhaps the deep water scares you, especially when you think of how vast and dark it can be.

Personally, I enjoy standing on the shore, marveling at the immensity of God's deep ocean of grace and truth. I feel the water creeping around my ankles as I slowly sink into the sand.

The beach graciously contours to my feet like no manmade shoe ever could. I could stand there for hours.

Wrestling with Questions

If you're like most people, all that we've said so far hasn't fully answered all your questions. You're not satisfied yet because this mystery of predestination still bothers you. It disturbs you (as it should) because you can't make all the puzzle pieces fit. I think that's a pretty normal response. You wonder what's the point of telling anyone about Jesus if the outcome has already been rigged. How can our choice of God be real and authentic if it is predestined? How can God choose me, but I also choose Him? How can two mutually exclusive truths both be equally true? If Jesus is really God (who *can't* sin), how could His temptation have been genuine? Doesn't accepting predestination lead to fatalism?

And while we're at it, what about the question of fairness? What does "God is fair" mean, and do I really want that? Do my ideas of fairness and equity stem from playground kickball rules that say that everybody gets a turn? That sounds like *fair* to me. And am I so entrenched with my own ideas of how things ought to be (or how God ought to be) that I am unwilling to admit that I don't know as much as I think I do? Does *fair* require God to treat every one of His rebellious creations equally? I mean, hasn't He read our Constitution?

Must my concept of fairness bow to the One in whose world we live and whose air we breathe? Should my definition yield to His? Is God messed up when it comes to fairness, or have we simply been unwilling to let Him have a free will? Is His will bound by our parameters, or is it the other way around? Do we really want God to be fair—for all people to be treated equitably and receive exactly and only what they deserve? Is it possible that for God to be fair, He'd be required to send us all to judgment?

Lying on my dorm room bed, it occurred to my 18-year-old mind that inherent to the concept of a Supreme Being would be the concession that some of His motives and means might be beyond us—beyond description, beyond understanding—but yet not beyond believing. The presence of faith and relationship enables mortals like you (and village idiots like me) to embrace things that don't make much sense.

That being said, it still doesn't answer all the questions concerning why God apparently chooses some but not others, but I'm pretty sure it has something to do with the "I'm God and you're not" principle. That still doesn't automatically lessen the shock of how predestination alters our view of God, self and life. I am still in process there. Maybe you are, too.

Do you have to believe in predestination in order to become a Christian? No. Do you have to believe in it to grow and be a good Christian? No. Will I think any less of you if you don't? Not a chance. Is it one of the most difficult truths you will ever wrestle with in your spiritual journey? Without a doubt.

Of all the mysteries we will discuss in this book, this one may cause you to scratch a sore spot into your head. In the end, you will have to work through this one yourself, wrestling with this disturbing concept and its confusing implications. From time to time, you'll need to lie on your bed and stare at the ceiling. You'll want to talk it through with others. You will definitely need to search through your Bible, asking God to give you His perspective on the whole thing. And when you come to your own conclusions, like me you'll still live with some unanswered questions.

* * *

After seeing the Rosetta Stone at the British Museum that day, I took the London tube over to the National Gallery, where some of the world's great masterpieces of art are housed. Rembrandt, Da Vinci, Monet, Van Gogh—they're all there. Some of them are larger than life, with a depth, texture and attention to detail that defies human understanding. Some of these masterpieces actually look like enlargements of photographs, too precise to have been brush-stroked by human hands. As I paused before each painting, pretending to know how to appreciate the work, I found myself at a loss for words, literally speechless in the presence of works so far beyond my ability to describe or figure out. Others may be able to, but not this boy. Way beyond merely seeing the expression of talent, I found myself encountering the *soul* of the painter through his artistic offering. I was in awe—and still am.

There's so much about predestination that still messes with my mind. As a result, I don't think I could, as some do, coldly proclaim this mystery of predestination in terms of some doctrinal math equation or systematized theological formula. For me, it's like gazing into a sunset, or breathing in the thin Colorado air while standing at the foot of the Rocky Mountains, or being stunned into silence by the beauty of a Botticelli. It's all too much. And I'm not sure what all it means.

Sort of like finding out I've been written into the will.

CHAPTER 4

THE TREASURE OF THE HIDDEN STORY

THE MYSTERY OF THE KINGDOM

*The knowledge of the secrets of the
kingdom of God has been given to you.*

Luke 8:10

Roaches scurry across the damp, concrete floor. Rats scuttle by, desperately searching for crumbs. It's dark and damp in the small cell, and the stench is nearly unbearable. Sitting for days in his own feces, Jeremiah Denton has bigger problems than a few cockroaches and rats. Denton's feet are confined in rusty iron stocks; his wrists are worn with blisters from handcuffs; and his two closest companions are Infection and Dysentery. Soldiers with machine guns stand guard outside the steel doors that separate him from freedom and light.

Welcome to Hoa Lo Prison, better known as the Hanoi Hilton. For seven and a half years, Jeremiah Denton, Jr., called this hellhole home. An unwitting guest of the North Vietnamese government, Denton was shot down while on a routine flying mission. Since that July morning in 1965, he survived on a diet consisting largely of bread and rice. Starvation loomed like a low-lying cloud over his body at all times, his once 170-pound frame reduced to a 120-pound emaciated shell of his former self.

He and his fellow American prisoners endured unimaginable horrors at the hands of their captors. Four of Denton's almost eight years at the Hanoi Hilton were spent in solitary confinement, robbing him of friendship and contact with other people. Subjected to unthinkable cruelty and regular beatings, his body was racked with scars and pain.

In his book *When Hell Was in Session*, Denton tells of being forced to participate in propaganda for the Vietnamese government. In made-for-television interviews, he was put under enormous pressure to denounce the United States and their involvement in the war.

Watching one of those staged television interviews in 1966, Naval Intelligence officers noticed something strange about Denton's eyes. He seemed to be blinking erratically, as if unusually bothered by the harsh lighting. But upon closer examination, they finally realized that Denton was blinking a covert message in Morse code: T-O-R-T-U-R-E. This, in spite of the fact that his captors had promised him more pain if he failed to fully cooperate. Denton's heroic and risky act was the first confirmation that American POWs in Vietnam were being tortured.

Jeremiah Denton was motivated to send a hidden message because he wanted to prevent his captors from understanding what he was saying. At the same time, he hoped and prayed that his friends back home would somehow get the message loud and clear. And they did. What was hidden from one became enlightenment to the other.

As I read the Bible, I notice that Jesus does this sometimes. Not blinking Morse code with His eyes, but speaking in code. Instead of speaking plainly like you think He would, He sometimes hides His message, particularly when speaking about His kingdom. But why all the veiled references? Why play hide-and-seek? Why not just speak plainly about it? Why be the cryptic Christ? Why all the mystery? Is He tossing out clues to some spiritual scavenger hunt? Is this Kingdom only for those clever enough to master the Master's metaphors? What do these stories mean? Is there a depth buried beneath His simplicity? And why did the One whose mission was to reveal God seem so often to be hiding Him from us? What is the mystery of His kingdom, and what does it have to do with me?

Parables for the People

During the first century, the Roman Empire ruled the known world. And because Rome was in charge, Rome made the rules. You lived in their territory, in their land, in their realm. You were under their dominion and had to abide by their laws. Their government was in charge. So when Jesus spoke the word "kingdom," everybody understood the concept, from personal experience.

But here's where Jesus' story takes a twist. Jesus wasn't talking about a Roman kingdom, but a spiritual and heavenly one, one that had nothing to do with Rome. And this concept got people's attention because He introduced the kingdom of God in a most unusual way—not through reading Bible verses or teaching formal lessons, but by telling stories.

Sounds kind of elementary, doesn't it? Sort of juvenile, like the way you might communicate to children—simply, with word pictures, metaphors, and such—not at all what you would expect from a prophet, priest or king.

Using these stories (or parables), Jesus compared God's kingdom to a man who sows good seed (see Matt. 13:24-30,36-43), a mustard seed (see Matt. 13:21-32; Mark 4:30-32; Luke 13:18-19), yeast (see Matt. 13:33; Luke 13:20-21), a king (see Matt. 18:23-35), a treasure (see Matt. 13:44), a merchant (see Matt. 13:45) and a net (see Matt. 13:47-50). It was imagery His audience should have instantly and uniquely understood . . . yet some still didn't get it. Instead they stood clueless, as if Jesus had spoken in some unknown tongue. So this kingdom of God remained a mystery to most, as if there were a filter scrambling the message:

[Jesus'] disciples came and asked him, "Why do you always tell stories when you talk to the people?"

Then he explained to them, "You are permitted to understand the secrets of the Kingdom of Heaven, but others are not. To those who are open to my teaching, more understanding will be given, and they will have an abundance of knowledge. But for those who are not listening, even what little understanding they have will be taken away from them. That is why I use these parables, for they look but they don't really see. They hear, but they don't really listen or understand. This fulfills the prophecy of Isaiah, which says:

'You will hear my words, but you will not understand; you will see what I do, but you will not comprehend. For the hearts of these people are hardened, and their ears cannot hear, and they have closed their eyes—so their eyes cannot see, and their ears cannot hear, and their hearts cannot understand, and they cannot turn to me and let me heal them' " (Matt. 13:10-15, *NLT*).

What does He mean by "the secrets of the Kingdom of Heaven," and why is He hiding them from people?

As Jesus drops clues in His parables, we discover there is both a present and a future aspect to God's kingdom (see Matt. 5:3; 6:10,33; 7:21; 11:12). Sometimes when Jesus talked about it, the Kingdom is here on Earth, and other times it's somewhere else. Sometimes the Kingdom is in heaven and other times it's in you (see Luke 17:21).

But why was the message of the Kingdom so cloudy to those original hearers of Jesus' words? To a Jew living in the first century, the idea of God's kingdom would have conjured up dreams of the day when Roman oppression was no more and God ruled the earth (see Dan. 2:44). Unfortunately, most of the Jews familiar with this idea were the religious teachers and leaders. And let's just say these guys, especially a group called the Pharisees, *had issues*. Their religious system was a well-oiled machine, and Jesus' revolutionary talk of a "kingdom within" was a thorn in their sides (see Luke 17:21).

Not one to be easily intimidated, Jesus' message to those teachers and leaders was threefold: (1) The future kingdom of God is not what you think it will be; (2) entrance requirements to this kingdom are not what you think they are; and (3) this new kingdom is more of a spiritual relationship than a physical place (see Matt. 5:3-20; 7:21; 18:3; Luke 10:9; 11:20; 17:20-21).

In other words, Jesus was saying, "You guys are not even close to God's heart on this issue." Jesus didn't deny God's future earthly reign, but the problem was that the Jewish leadership put such a tremendous emphasis on abiding by external rituals and rules that they subverted a spiritual, inner relationship with God. In other words, they were stuck in a certain way of viewing God, and Jesus radically challenged that perspective. They thought they possessed the secret formula and had God stuff all figured out.

Christ burst the bubble of their good-ol'-boy system. And because of His new, out-of-the-box approach, the religious elite were unwilling to hear Him. They were too proud, smug and satisfied with their traditions and the power they exercised over the people. They had their version of the Kingdom going on, one where they were in charge. Swollen with the pride of their own egos, they had no place for fresh thoughts about ancient truth, no room for any new perspective about God—not even if God's Son was the One bringing it.

Sadly, I see a similar thing happening today. I'm talking about people in the Church who are married to the same tired old traditions, who have "always done it that way." These people feel threatened by new ideas and fresh views and interpretations. New songs or expressions of worship are dismissed as shallow or unbiblical. New approaches to seeing God in nontraditional ways are condemned and written off as liberal or New Age, as if God only spoke to His Church *back then*. They associate changing communication style with denying truth itself.

It's the same attitude that has kept people in spiritual darkness for centuries. It's an attitude that says, "We already know everything about God and life." To these people, there's nothing new to learn or experience. Traditional ways of seeing God or doing church are guarded like a bank vault, and no one is allowed entrance . . . not even God. You probably know some of these folks. They'd sooner die than change or admit they're wrong. Anything new or different is bad. Maybe that's what Jesus meant when He spoke of how difficult it was to pour new wine into old wineskins (see Mark 2:22).

That's the kind of people Jesus is dealing with here. And it was their unwillingness to hear Him and His new ideas about God's kingdom that motivated the Son of God to hide it from them. Their stubbornness blinded them to simple truth and the new thing His Spirit was doing. So Jesus said, "Hey, My kingdom is different from the one you're expecting, and unless you change, you're not getting in" (see Mark 10:15).

An Inside Job

So what are these simple secrets of the Kingdom Jesus spoke of? What are the differences between the Kingdom Jesus talked about and the kingdom that His generation expected?

> Once, having been asked by the Pharisees when the kingdom of God would come, Jesus replied, "The kingdom of God does not come with your careful observation, nor will people say, 'Here it is,' or 'There it is,' because the *kingdom of God is within you*" (Luke 17:20-21, emphasis added).

Humble entrance to a Kingdom within—ah, there's the mystery. Consider that those words were spoken to a generation of worshipers whose understanding of God revolved around the Temple. Worship was very much location-centered. They worshiped at the Temple because that was the place God had promised to make His presence dwell (see Deut. 12:11; Ps. 132:13-14; Acts 7:44-49). For them, the Temple was *the* focal point of the Jewish God experience (like most other religions in those days). Everything of major spiritual significance happened on the Temple grounds. So here comes Jesus, introducing an old concept that seemed completely new, a fresh take on an old paradigm, a re-establishment of the agreement-relationship between God and humans. It would have nothing to do with a building.

God was moving on to better things. You can see how this suggestion radically challenged conventional religious thinking of the day. Few religious leaders had ever conceived of God's kingdom in this way before. Jesus' new idea not only challenged their approach to religion, but it also messed with their entire worldview. And they killed Him for it.

I wonder if it's so different today. I live in a city where one church just completed a $40 million building, and another is about to build a facility costing over $55 million! You ever thought about how much cash that is? To put it in perspective, if your annual salary is $75,000, it would take you 733 years to earn that much money! Of course, money is a relative thing, right? What is normal to one may be extravagant to another. But hey, let's spend tens of millions just so we can worship in comfort, conveniently secluded from our less wealthy neighbors. Hmm.

Forgive my ranting, but somewhere along the way we got sidetracked and lost our way. Have we become like those first-century Pharisees? Have we missed the point? Have we overshot the runway? Have we, under the guise of excellence, fallen into the trap of affluent extravagance? Have we traded a revolutionary faith for a Family Life Center?

In America when we say the word "church," we immediately think of street addresses and architecture. Our society's mental picture of God has been reduced to real estate, largely because the focus of today's Church is centered around what's happening *at the church*. Meetings, Bible studies, conferences, midweek services, training seminars, choir practice, youth meetings—everything happens *at the church*. Success is often measured by how many warm bodies cross the threshold each week and how many activities are listed in the church bulletin. If this kind of location-centered activity goes on long enough, we begin to associate the church building with the Church itself. Our identity becomes an inanimate object. The most often asked phrase is "Where do you go to church?" It's all about the building and what's happening at "God's House." It's the Temple thing all over again. I wonder what our identity would be if the Church had no permanent location or if we only used the building once a week. Is a modern-day reincarnation of Temple-centered worship what Jesus had in mind when He was dying on the cross? Is the Church of today what He intended Her to become?

Are we really growing in our experience of God's kingdom, or are high-profile pastors simply building little kingdoms of their own? What would happen if our megachurches split themselves into smaller, community-based congregations with pastors who knew the names of the flock and whose members had authentic relationships with one another? I wonder how society's concept of Church would change then.

Once when I was a pastor at one of those megachurches, my son Davis bolted out of the sanctuary after the morning service and was soon racing across the huge foyer (the one with a marble floor imported from Italy), probably on his way to scavenge leftover donuts from adult Sunday School rooms. Suddenly, an elderly woman stopped him dead in his tracks. Holding out her hand like a traffic cop, she scolded him, "Young man, you shouldn't run in God's House!"

Without missing a beat, Davis looked up at her and innocently replied, "But, ma'am, this isn't God's House." Then he pointed to his heart and said, "*This* is God's House." And he continued on his donut hunt. Not running, but walking—with style. (Later we told Davis not to run in church so that he wouldn't accidentally knock over elderly ladies.)

Today, as in Jesus' day, we still focus largely on the external. It's all about activities *at* the church instead of what's happening *in* the Church when She's outside the building. Outward appearance too often takes priority over transparency, authenticity and spirituality. We're more intentional and excited about commissioning plans for a new facility instead of Christ's command to *be the Church out in the world*. In short, we have become self-absorbed. That wouldn't be so much of a problem, but everyone is watching. We're on display before an observant world. Christian culture has become all about *us*—our wants, our needs, our expectations—and our consumer-driven addiction is consuming the Church. (And we wonder why a new generation of adolescents and young adults struggle to connect with the present-day Church.)

Contrast this current "kingdom thinking" with Jesus' words:

I tell you the truth, unless a kernel of wheat falls to the ground and dies, it remains only a single seed. But if it dies, it produces many seeds. The man who loves his life will lose it, while the man who hates his life in this world will keep it for eternal life (John 12:24-25).

A Jesus-kingdom mindset means we think of others before ourselves. It means exchanging self-indulgence for service to others. It means we give more than we get. It means we create a new image, re-inventing our image of Church. It means we put to death the self-absorbed, bloated Jabba-the-Hut monster that has been consuming the contemporary Church.

Jesus ran into a brick wall when He suggested that God's kingdom had more to do with the heart than it did with the Temple or a physical overthrow of Rome. It's not hard to imagine that He would tell Christians today to stop building those massive church buildings and spend their money on efforts that actually change the world and help people.

Sounds extreme, doesn't it? Think of the blank stares you would receive if you suggested this course of action. Imagine the ridicule, the rationalization, the opposition. You might even be labeled a radical, maybe even un-Christian, ungodly, a traitor to God.

Yeah, you and Jesus.

A Mystical Mystery

This new Kingdom idea Jesus spoke of was no doubt a mystery to the religious crowd. They just didn't get it, but not because they were intellectually challenged. According to Jesus, they weren't open to letting God out of the box they had placed Him in. They had God all figured out. There was no mystery. They already had God's Word mastered, even memorizing His rules (along with adding a few hundred meticulous ones of their own). But Jesus said He wouldn't reveal the secrets of God's kingdom to anyone who wasn't open to His teaching (see Matt. 13:12). Those people desperately needed to buy a vowel, call a lifeline or at least wake up and smell the coffee.

Let's put our spiritual protest signs down for a minute and ask ourselves a critical question: How open are *we* to Jesus' teachings?

Forget about the corporate Christian giants. What about you and me? Are we ready to receive Jesus' radical interpretation of the Kingdom? Not our remixed version, not our culturally overdubbed edition, but the pure, undiluted, original teachings of God's Son? And what if they clash with our current template of the kingdom? Are we willing to rethink our present Western, American evangelical approach to God? Are we willing to put aside our preconceived notions of Christianity and trade them in for God's fresh perspective? Are we ready for that? Could we handle it?

It's possible that part of the problem we have with this whole Kingdom thing is that we don't live in one. We live in a representative democracy. In a democracy, we can disagree with and dethrone our leaders. If God's not the ruler we want Him to be, we'll just vote Him out in the next election. (Outside the coffee shop where I write these words, demonstrators stage weekly protests against our current president's foreign policies. Power to the people, right?) Words like "king" and "kingdom" invoke images of evil dictators ruling countries with iron fists. Or at best, we think of benign monarchies where the sovereign is more of a figurehead than a ruler. So it's a bit of a stretch to think about God's kingdom, especially one that exists in the here and now.

For Christians, maybe in the absence of God's visible kingdom, we feel obliged to create our own—corporately and personally. But are we willing to let our hearts be His throne and for His kingdom to come in us? Are we Christians who enjoy giving God our opinion, or are we humble followers willing to rethink life itself from His perspective? Are we open to Jesus' secret of the Kingdom to be revealed to us today? Can we accept the truth that the King doesn't only dwell in a high and holy place but right here and now *in* us? We may embrace the privilege of bypassing priest and pastor and dealing directly with the King ourselves, but is the King allowed to rule from within us? *That* is extreme thinking from a revolutionary mind.

But here's where the mystery takes another mystical turn in the road. We can *see* our pastor, just as Jews living in Jesus' day could see the priests, scribes and Temple. And their sacrifices were tangible, measurable, concrete, physical—real. But Jesus' new concept of God's kingdom emphasized a reality more invisible, ethereal, immaterial—*out there*. You can't reach out and grab this Kingdom like you can an offering plate or a hymnal. It's not real like a steeple or the veil of the Temple (see Matt. 27:51). It's not as concrete as the rules handed down from the Pharisees or the prohibitions prescribed for you by modern-day Christendom. It's much simpler to shun all R-rated movies than it is to evaluate all movies through an inner relationship with the unseen God. Who needs God when you have a list of rules to guide you?

It's religion based on rules that Jesus was correcting. It's the old way of thinking He came to replace. In the Old Testament, God's law was concrete and specific for a people under an old covenant. Like children, God's people needed detailed instructions regarding most everything (see Gal. 3:23-4:3). But Jesus fulfilled all the requirements of the old law for us. Now, in

Christ we are children who cry out more for relationship than rules (see Gal. 4:6-7). We no longer follow the old operating system. Jesus took us from MS-DOS to OSX or Vista. He took us by the hand, leading us into a *new* testament. From physical to spiritual. External to internal. Law to grace.

Still, the problem with having God's kingdom within us is that we can't actually see this King. Or audibly hear Him for that matter. That's part of this deep mystery. But remember, in its infancy, Christianity was much more mystical than it is now. It was largely faith dependent; rather than relying on a long history of teaching and Bible study, it had a daily Spirit dependence. Sure, the Early Church had its share of problems. And She struggled with those problems for several hundred years, until She matured some. But being young doesn't automatically infer immaturity. In the beginnings of any great movement, there can also be clear vision, passion, fervency, a willingness to sacrifice for the cause, deep commitment, innocence and a fresh, daily dependence on the principles on which it is founded. This is something future generations can lose as they allow the weeds to grow up, choking the original vision that motivated them and gave them their cutting-edge distinction.

Jesus felt very good leaving His disciples under the care and leadership of the Holy Spirit. Think of how it must have rocked their world when Jesus told them He was leaving them (see John 14:1-2). They had been used to having Him with them at all times. They had grown comfortable with enjoying the physical presence of Christ—someone they could see, hear and touch (see 1 John 1:1). Now He was telling them He wouldn't see them for a very long time. Instead, He promised to send them someone else to take His place (see John 14:16-17). This someone (the Holy Spirit), though equal to Jesus in every way, could not be—unlike Him—seen and touched. But how could God, whose presence has dwelt in the Temple's holy of holies all this time, now suddenly transfer His permanent residence to our physical bodies (see 1 Cor. 6:19)? And where exactly would He live? In our minds? Hearts? Liver? Kidneys? How does that part of the Kingdom work? How do you relate to a God with whom you have no tangible association?

By nature we are such physical beings, accustomed to interpreting life through our physical senses—sight, smell, sound, touch and taste. We're experts in recognizing the smell of grilling burgers, the sound of a baby's cry, the taste of an apple or the feel of soft sheets. But when it comes to God and His kingdom, Jesus asks us to change templates, adding a fresh new facet to our relationship with Him. He asks us to engage our spirit, to go beyond merely believing in what we can see. In short, He asks His followers to begin learning how to sense Him. *That's* the mysticism we're so uncomfortable with. And understandably so. It's like suddenly being required to write with the opposite hand. We're not used to that. It will be awkward and will take some time getting used to. Honestly, this subjective, mystical element of faith frightens us a little, doesn't it? Sounds too much like Eastern philosophy, right? Like we're supposed to sit in the lotus position, eyes closed, and meditate while repeating some mindless chant. Freaky, weird stuff.

I'm with you. But keep in mind, Jesus introduced this mystical Kingdom concept to a first-century Middle Eastern audience, where many Eastern philosophies originated. Mysticism was more familiar to their culture than it is to ours. It's not that Jesus ever intended us to disengage or disconnect from Scripture. The Bible (whose mystery we'll discuss in chapter 7) is our immovable anchor and confident plumb line of unchanging truth. It is one of the few concrete, visible, touchable connections we actually have to God. It's His Word, true in every way. But it's not God Himself. That's why we have to be careful not to worship it as a physical object. With Scripture as our guide, Jesus spoke of a mystical kingdom of God within us, namely the unique relationship His disciples would have with His Holy Spirit. It's a relationship Paul would talk more about in his writings.

Consider some of the things God says are true of this mysterious, invisible Holy Spirit habitating in us: He teaches us all things, gives us the words to speak when we face opposition, speaks to others through us, helps us pray, harmonizes His desires with ours, gives us power to overcome, guides us through life, communicates with our spirit regarding our relationship to God, interacts with our thoughts, causes us to experience intimacy with God the Father, and rules in us (see Matt. 13:11; John 14:16-17; Rom. 8:5-6,13-14,16,26; 9:1; 1 Cor. 12:13; Eph. 5:18). He can also be made to feel sadness (see Eph. 4:30). He is personal, subjective and mystical.

And correct me if I'm wrong, but that sure sounds like a real relationship to me. The portrait Scripture paints of this invisible, intangible Kingdom within us doesn't sound very unreal but seems practical, concrete and more authentic than most relationships between people you can see and touch. It's just that in such a physical, tangible culture as ours, God has called us to relate to a Spirit we can't see!

Meeting God in a Witch Shop

There's great mystery here. Even with all this certainty of God's internal kingdom, it's still not as easily recognizable or visible as a church building or the White House. Yet it's just as real. In fact, it's *more* real. Long after our church buildings have crumbled into the dust or been replaced by new, bigger church structures, our inner connection to God's kingdom will remain. Sadly, many who don't ascribe to Christianity have tapped into this inner Kingdom idea better than some Christ followers.

In my neighborhood, not far from my home is a store called the Broom Closet. At first I thought it was a cleaning-supply company. Later I discovered it was a witch shop, a business dedicated to the promotion of Wicca and other pagan religions. With my curiosity aroused, I naturally wanted to know more, so I went and checked it out. Inside, I found herbs, potions, amulets, jewelry, candles, books and paraphernalia related to Wicca and paganism. From one rack, I picked up a pamphlet and read these words: "Unlike many traditional religions who worship once a week in a church building, pagans worship every day, enjoying a continual intimacy with the god(s) within them."

After reading that pamphlet, my jaw dropped—not because I was harboring a secret desire to start a fire with my new demonic literature or feeling self-righteous because I knew the truth . . . I felt sharply rebuked. I was angry that this inner intimacy had been hijacked by fallen spirits, but I also felt ashamed that Christians and Christendom had portrayed our God as someone to visit once a week, like paying respects to a dying great aunt. I was embarrassed that we are perceived by many as people who compartmentalize our faith. We may carry a moral code with us the other six days of the week, but the Master Himself is still viewed as "up there" in heaven. Rather than tapping into self-energy or vibrations from nature or Celtic gods and goddesses, Jesus' kingdom is *the presence of the one true God*. There's a big difference between the "god within" and the "God within."

Standing in that Wicca shop, I made a spiritual decision to work toward changing that perception, to make a difference in people's thinking about Christians and the Church. Don't misunderstand: I'm not launching a campaign against construction of church buildings or using money to buy stuff for ministry. But my desire is that when your city thinks about your church, what comes to mind are faces and loving actions, not merely a piece of real estate.

In that way, we can influence our world's perspective of God's kingdom, erasing the empire-building mentality that has eaten us alive.

* * *

So what now? With this new outlook on the Kingdom, how do I sense the Holy Spirit within my spirit? How do I hear Him? How do I know He's leading? How do I sense His presence within? How do I train my spirit to daily interact with His? Is it more than just memorizing Bible verses? How do I have a relationship with the Spirit living in me?

Can I let go of my current Christian crutches and step into the spiritual realm where God is? Am I creating a comfortable place for His Spirit to make a home in me? Am I willing to relearn what it means to walk by faith? Can I put the old operating system out on the curb for pickup and adopt God's new revolutionary way of Kingdom living?

Or will I miss Jesus the next time He blinks in code?

CHAPTER 5

THE MIDNIGHT VISITOR

THE MYSTERY OF PRAYER

*If you believe, you will receive whatever
you ask for in prayer.*
Matthew 21:22

I had never been arrested before, never known what it felt like to be placed in handcuffs and led away to jail. But I had an eerie premonition that I was about to find out. County jail didn't stir up pleasant images in my mind. In my town, a lot of backwoods boys were arrested for doing things like setting barns on fire, shooting road signs or playing cruel tricks on animals. The thought of rooming with a bunch like that made me nauseous when I thought of what they might do to a city boy like me. But I prepared for the worst anyway.

It was Friday night, and I was 16. Just days earlier, I had made a decision to become a follower of Jesus. I had very little knowledge of what it meant to be a Christian. I was a total rookie. The whole Jesus thing was so new to me that I'm not sure I could have told you how to become a Christian had you asked me. All I knew was that I had a new lease on life and that I was going to heaven one day. God came along at just the right time, filling the empty space in my heart and rescuing me from certain disaster.

I played in a rock band in those days. We were sort of a hybrid of Southern rock meets the Beatles meets Led Zeppelin— an odd combination, but then again, so were we. So this particular Friday night, we were playing at a dance following the local football game, when, in the middle of a song, several South Carolina State Troopers burst through the back door of the auditorium. Assuming they weren't there to dance, I began to worry—and for good cause. They were headed straight for me! That's when my mind went blank, and I forgot which chords to play. The troopers proceeded through the crowd and up onto the stage, where, to my surprise, they walked past me and forcibly grabbed our lead guitarist, leading him out the door. Talk about awkward moments! I nervously informed the audience we'd be right back after a short break. Once outside, I discovered that some marijuana had been found in the glove compartment of his car.

"Great!" I lamented to our drummer. "Now what are we gonna do? We still have another set to play."

Returning back inside the building, I was walking back toward the stage when a thought popped into my head, *Why don't you ask God to help?*

In the days since becoming a Christian, I didn't recall having prayed for anything yet. I didn't even know how. But what did I have to lose? So I cried out in desperation, "God, please don't let them take our guitarist away. We really need him tonight."

And that was that. I wasn't trying to impress God with Christian lingo—I didn't know any. I didn't even know to say "in Jesus' name." It was simply a request for help. But no sooner had I finished praying then our lead guitarist walked inside the gymnasium and up onto the stage. Picking up his guitar, he turned to me and said, "Let's go, man. Let's play." As if nothing had happened.

"Excuse me," I said. "What happened out there? I thought you were under arrest."

"I was," he said. "But the weirdest thing just happened. For some strange reason, right before taking me away, somebody else walked up and told the troopers that the marijuana belonged to him and that he had put it in my car. So they took the handcuffs off me and put 'em on him. What do you think about that?"

Honestly, I didn't know what to think. I only knew that within 30 seconds of praying, I had an answer—a first-ever answer to prayer—and that amazed me.

Fast-forward to about a year ago, while driving home from Dallas with my wife. We were discussing the needs of our ministry, when I said, "You know what we really need? We need God to tell someone to invest some big bucks in our ministry."

"That would be great," she responded.

And so, driving down Highway 30, I prayed out loud.

"God," I said, "I'd like you to just speak to someone directly today. And I'd like You to tell someone these words: 'Write Jeff the check right now.'"

Two days later, while opening the mail, I discovered a card from a dear friend with whom I'd had very little contact in the past 10 years. This person told of how she had heard of what we were currently doing in our ministry, and while thinking about us, God suddenly spoke to her spirit and said these words: "Write Jeff the check right now."

Enclosed was a check for a large sum of money.

After my screaming and shouting subsided and my wife's tears dried, I could only sit in wonder that God had done such a thing. He had spoken to my friend at the same time that I had prayed. And it all happened as a direct result of prayer.

That's what I'm talking about. But in case you think that kind of stuff happens to me a lot, let me quickly say that there have also been seasons when virtually none of my requests have been granted. Zero. This causes me to wonder about the randomness of prayer.

And the mystery of it.

Fore!

When you think about it, being able to communicate with our Creator is kind of an eerie concept. And it seems even more bizarre when you consider that He's invisible. I once saw a movie about a man who had daily conversations with an imaginary six-foot-tall rabbit named Harvey. People looked at the man as if he were loopy. I wonder if that's what some people think of Christians when they talk to God. Are we loopy, too?

Truth is, lots of people pray—people of all religions. They expect (or at least hope) there's somebody up there who's listening. Radical Islamic militants cry out to Allah after beheading their enemies. Hindus pray to a multitude of gods. And Christians pray to Jesus. Sometimes the Muslim gets what is asked for and the Christian gets nothing but silence. (Explain that one to your skeptical, unbelieving friend.) And why is it that when you're living a near-perfect life, your prayers fall flat? Then at other times, you're barely scraping by in life, struggling with temptation and sin, and God comes through in a big way?

We think we know what prayer is, but do we? Haven't you ever wondered why some of your prayers pay off while others seem to get lost in the mail? Has trying to figure out how the whole prayer thing works ever bothered you? And why does it frighten you so much to even think about praying in public?

Of course, people pray in church. Public prayer is a regular part of most church services and the congregation is expected to bow their heads and close their eyes. Once I peeked during such a prayer, only to discover there were all kinds of activity going on besides prayer. I later learned that this prayer time was really a cover for choir members to have sufficient time to stealthily make it back to their seats without anyone noticing.

Prayers at athletic events have always confused me. For example, opposing church softball teams pray together on the field before a game and then, immediately after prayer, look up and say "Good luck!" to one another. Then they usually proceed to play as if there were no God in heaven at all. But I thought praying to God meant you didn't believe in luck. Who's in control—God or luck?

Or what about when high school football players stand on their respective sidelines during the closing moments of a close game, each side praying for God to let them win. How does the Lord decide who wins in those situations? Or does He stand back and just let them play it out?

Why does answered prayer seem so random? It's almost like putting four quarters in a drink machine but never knowing if a soda will appear or if the machine will eat your money.

The arbitrary nature of prayer is a huge part of the mystery here. But you might expect as much, seeing as how the Bible does mention certain conditions for answered prayer. God lists a bunch of reasons why He *won't* grant our requests:

- When we "ask with wrong motives" (Jas. 4:3)
- When we refuse to forgive someone (see Mark 11:25)
- When we don't treat our wives "with respect" (1 Pet. 3:7)
- When there is sin in our hearts (see Ps. 66:18)
- When we fail to ask in faith (see Matt. 21:21-22)
- When we don't pray according to God's will (see 1 John 5:14-15)

Hey, that's a lot to remember. How do you know if you've done all the right things before you approach God in prayer?

It reminds me of when my father-in-law (an avid golfer) individually took my three boys out for golf lessons, hoping they would adopt the sport. As a result, two of them play football and the third jokingly says, "Sports are for nerds." Not one of them will touch a golf club. The reason? They hate golf.

Returning home from Granddad's golf lessons, they'd each collapsed into a pile, exhausted and complaining about how complicated the game was. Their grandfather had filled their heads with all the things you have to remember before hitting a golf ball: "Stand up straight. Bend your legs. Lift your chin. Align your feet. Position the ball. Watch your swing path. Check the wind. Lean forward. Look down. Open your stance. Loosen your grip. Concentrate. Check your target. Lean back. Square your shoulders. Straighten your arms. . . . Now relax and hit the ball!"

That's way too much to remember before you even make contact with the ball. To my boys, golf was no longer a game; it was Introduction to Quantum Physics!

You can see how prayer might appear this way to some. Trying to check off all the things you're supposed to avoid may scare a lot of people away from enjoying the game. You may also unconsciously get the impression that answered prayer is a matter of accumulating prayer points, sort of like a "buy three get one free" coupon.

Did God design prayer to be that way? Does He enjoy seeing us jump through spiritual hoops? Do we have to wait for the planets to align before we can be confident of getting what we ask for? If not, then just what are the rules of engagement in prayer? And why is it that when we fail to meet all of the previously listed conditions, God still answers our prayers sometimes? What's up with that? What does it say about prayer?

Prayer can seem like a religious Rubik's Cube—complicated. But maybe God never intended it to be this way. Could it be that the mystery of prayer is made more so by our attempt to figure it out?

There's no denying the fact that prayer involves asking God for things—needs, wants, requests, and so on. But this can become the tail that wags the dog. Could there be a simpler purpose for conversing with the Most High?

Honest to God

If the main purpose of prayer isn't to get stuff from God, then what is prayer, really? Confession? Adoration? Thanksgiving? Some cheesy acrostic? These are all worthy topics to address in prayer. But is there something else He wants from us?

A clue may be found in Jesus' words to His disciples. They asked Him to teach them how to pray. He began by encouraging them to address God as *Father*. Not *Eternal One, Sovereign Lord* or *Almighty King*, though He is all these things. When given a chance to imprint our minds with a mental tattoo of who God is, Jesus requested that we call Him *Father*.

"Father" communicates connection, bloodline, affinity, relationship . . . intimacy. It means there's history between you and the One you're talking to. The word implies a strong dependence. There is deep respect, but no fear (see Luke 11:2; 1 John 4:18), submission, but not slavery (see Matt. 6:10). More than anything, though, it defines the context in which we pray. It means we can reverence God without being bound by religious formalities. It means we can touch His heart without getting hung up on rituals or formulas.

"Father" means there's freedom to approach God without fear of condemnation, confident that grace will flow from His throne (see Heb. 4:16; 10:19). "Father" also communicates a freedom to be yourself before God. As we saw in the last chapter, He's *in* you already. And He's there *for* you.

Prayer is not like walking into the principal's office to reveal that it was you who started the fire in the boy's bathroom. Or like appearing before a traffic court judge to plead guilty for doing 83 mph in a 35-mph zone. Hey, He already knows what you've done. More important, He knows *you*—perfectly. Your prayers never reveal any new information to God. You don't report to God so that He can be clued in on the day's activities. Because He's already privy to all the dirt on you (and yet loves you anyway), it makes sense to simply be transparent with Him. You can tell Him anything, even expressing sorrow and regret for the selfish, sinful things you've said, thought or done. And, in case you're wondering, God doesn't expect you to remember all the stuff you've done wrong.

Of all the things God values, honesty is certainly near the top of the list. You can live holy and be self-righteous about it— and God is definitely *not* a fan of self-righteousness—but if you're transparent and (dare I say it) naked before Him about self, sin and life, there is a free flow to your relationship with Him (see Heb. 4:13). In other words, fewer dropped calls. And that makes God smile.

This freedom in prayer also means you aren't controlled by the expectations of a religious subculture. In other words, you don't have to close your eyes, bow your head, drop to your knees, end with "in Jesus' name" or even say "Amen." You also don't have to feel the pressure to say grace before a meal or impress others with your prayers. Having God as your Father removes the usual stress associated with prayer. The result is that you actually *want* to talk with God more.

Several years ago, I was a part of an extended prayer gathering. There were about 20 of us who had come to this little chapel on a local college campus. After spending about an hour in prayer, we headed into a second hour. That's when I noticed my friend Al. Laid out on the pew in front of me, Al had fallen fast asleep. I mean this brother was *gone*. In fact, he looked like a corpse in a coffin, lying on his back with arms folded neatly over his chest. And he was snoring . . . loudly.

I tried waking him up, but it only caused him to snort and shift to his side. Fortunately, his snoring eventually subsided and he dove into a much deeper, coma-like sleep. The rest of us continued praying for another hour. By that time it was about 10 P.M. and my stomach reminded me I hadn't fed it yet.

Now the noise from my growling stomach began to replace Al's snoring. And with my eyes also closed, I began fading in and out of consciousness. I was suspended between this world and a sort of dreamscape existence. It's that netherworld experience when you can hear what's going on around you, but you're also still dreaming. I had a bizarre string of those semi-awake episodes, interrupted only by periodic body jolts and rumblings in my gut.

After a while, the prayer suddenly halted, like a lull in the storm. Complete silence filled the chapel. I awoke long enough to think to myself, *Maybe this is it. Maybe we're done. I can go and eat now. Yes!* But my hope was short-lived when some guilt-driven prayer warrior took that silence as a sign that we were supposed to continue into yet another long session of prayer. At this point, I actually began praying to God for the prayers to end! And I suspect a percentage of those still awake were silently agreeing with me.

Eventually—and it was a long eventually—we did finish, after which I inhaled an entire pizza.

You may have had similar prayer experiences. Or you may think less of me (and Al) for falling asleep. After all, Jesus spent the entire night in prayer (see Luke 6:12). And we're supposed to do what Jesus would do, right? WWJD? (Hey, He walked on water, too.)

Today, I bear no permanent scars from my prayer marathon. I still participate in special prayer gatherings. And such times can be a healthy experience for a couple, a small group or an entire church.

But prayer can't be reserved only for special times of the day or week. That's like saying I only have a relationship with my wife when I'm out on a date with her. If that's all we have, then our relationship is pretty shallow, compartmentalized and sporadic. In reality, I talk with my wife all the time, every day. We have coffee in the mornings. I call her during the day. We take regular long walks together and discuss everything together. We do life together because we're close, spending lots of time in each other's company. So when we do go on a date, that's just one tiny expression of who we are. I think prayer ought to be like that. It has to flavor our lives for it to be a natural and organic part of who we are. It's not just a piece of the pie—it's the taste you get in every bite.

Having said that, I had always been bothered by the verse that says to "pray without ceasing" (1 Thess. 5:17, *NASB*). Taking that verse at face value, I thought it sounded impractical and unrealistic, and I wondered how God could possibly expect us to pray nonstop. My thoughts would rewind to that campus prayer time and a sense of dread would fill me (and my stomach would growl, too). I concluded that if praying without ceasing was what made a good Christian, I would never be one.

But then I began filtering verses like that through the lens of relationship. It was only then that those conditions we talked about earlier began making sense. It became clear that things like selfishness and unforgiveness affected my prayers mainly because they interrupted my relationship with God, like interrupting a conversation.

I also saw all Bible verses about prayer in the greater context of being with the Father. Suddenly, I imagined that praying without ceasing was like keeping my cell phone on and with me at all times: It was like having the ability to connect with God instantly at any time.

Prayer, for me, has become more than a way to just talk to God. I began by thinking my thoughts to Him, involving Jesus in the daily, practical things that were going on in my life. With honesty and love for Him as my motivation, I learned how to open up about my thoughts, dreams, desires, hurts, goals, failures, frustrations and sins—everything that makes up *me*.

Sometimes I get lost in telling God how awesome He is. Other times I'm filing complaints because of the cruddy day I'm having or because things didn't turn out like I had planned. I am now not afraid to tell Him exactly what I feel—anger, lust, joy, bitterness, disappointment, panic, fear, desperation or anticipation. It all flows through me and to Him. I think God likes that. And I am discovering prayer as a way for God's presence to grow in my life.

It Never Hurts to Ask

"Honesty" and "access": two words that make the mystery of prayer bearable to me. But another important word is "humility." I'm not talking about the "I'm a worthless worm" theology, the attitude that causes you to cower before the Creator in shame and fear, asking for a tiny morsel to drop from heaven's table. On the contrary, you have enormous worth in God's eyes. He created you. You are made in His image. God loves you. Christ died for you. His Spirit lives in you. You're status has been upgraded to righteous. You are His child. A worm is the last thing that comes to God's mind when He thinks of you. He thinks of you as a priceless work of art, "the apple of his eye" (Zech. 2:8). He has sworn to never forget you (see Isa. 49:15). The love God has for His own Son is the love He has for you (see John 17:26).

Knowing God thinks this way makes us feel grateful, and that gratitude gives birth to humility. A first cousin to honesty, humility involves being sincere about voluntarily surrendering to your Father. In light of everything He's done, it just feels like the right thing to do. It's this beautiful surrender that Jesus values so much (see Luke 18:10-14). But we don't do it in order to be accepted by God—we do it because we're already unconditionally accepted by Him.

It is in light of this relationship with God that He asks us to do something: He wants us to pray and ask Him for things. Big things, impossible things—anything (see Matt. 17:20-21; 18:19; 21:21-22). After all, we only ask for help when we can't do it ourselves, right? Prayer is a place where we ask for help.

One month before my conversion to Christianity, I was driving home from a friend's house late one rainy Sunday afternoon. My buddy Russell was with me. As we descended a hill on a lonely country road, I looked up to see a guy on a motorcycle coming around the bend toward us. Suddenly, and for no apparent reason, the motorcyclist lost control and went into a slide. Violently thrown from his bike, he rolled across the pavement and into a ditch, where he lay motionless. However, his motorcycle kept coming toward me, slamming into my door at about 40 mph. The impact of the crash sent glass spraying across my face and all over the car. Instinctively stomping on the brakes, I began a long skid down the hill on the wet pavement, eventually coming to rest in the ditch.

Momentarily dazed, I was snapped out of my shock when Russell shouted, "Jeff, you're on top of him! You're on top of him!"

Realizing that the weight of my car was crushing this man, I quickly reversed gears and backed up. On the road again, I now had another problem: My door had been wedged shut by the impact of the motorcycle crashing into it. Barefoot and with glass everywhere, I began kicking at my door in an attempt to open it.

I began to pray. "God, please don't let this man be dead! Please don't let him die! God, please help!"

For some reason, the words "manslaughter" and "jail" popped into my mind (you already know how I feel about jail). Prayer to me at that time was like dialing 9-1-1, like a fire alarm that you pull only in case of emergency. When there's a crisis or a fire, it's great to know you can pull the prayer alarm, right?

Finally kicking my door open, Russell and I raced down the wet road, only to discover the motorcyclist picking himself up from the ditch . . . without a single scratch on him! Not one. Now you could say he had a lucky slide across the pavement. You could also claim the ground was wet and absorbed the weight of the car. You could say my car, a classic VW bug, didn't weigh that much. You could claim that by the time the car stopped, the impact was minimal. You could say anything you like.

I say it was a direct answer to prayer.

I've learned that like any good father, God enjoys giving good things to His kids. Secular psychologists talk about the positive emotional impact of saying more yeses than nos to your kids' requests. God obviously understands that, too. He wants us to keep asking Him for things and not give up until we get what we want.

A woman once asked Jesus to rescue her daughter from demon possession, and Jesus answered her with silence. But she persisted until Jesus finally did what she asked. He then told her she had great faith (see Matt. 15:21-28). Another time, a Roman official approached Jesus, asking Him to heal his servant who was sick at home. Jesus agreed to come to his home and heal him. But the man asked Jesus to just say the word and that would be enough. And Jesus answered his request immediately. He too was praised for having great faith (see Matt. 8:5-13).

Jesus also told a story about someone who showed up at a friend's door at midnight and asked for three loaves of bread (you can imagine how inconvenient that would be):

> "Friend, lend me three loaves of bread, because a friend of mine on a journey has come to me, and I have nothing to set before him."
>
> Then the one inside answers, "Don't bother me. The door is already locked, and my children are with me in bed. I can't get up and give you anything." I tell you, though he will not get up and give him the bread because he is his friend, yet because of the man's boldness he will get up and give him as much as he needs.
>
> So I say to you: Ask and it will be given to you; seek and you will find; knock and the door will be opened to you. For everyone who asks receives; he who seeks finds; and to him who knocks, the door will be opened (Luke 11:5-10).

Keep in mind, Jesus told this story immediately after giving the disciples the now-famous Lord's Prayer model. The obvious lesson Jesus wants us to learn? Come to God for any reason at any time and don't stop knocking until He opens the door.

Does that sound sort of strange to you? It does to me. It sounds almost rude to be that persistent with God. But Jesus' story teaches us that eventually the door will open—if you keep knocking. And why? Because unlike your pajama-clad, grumpy, sleepy friend, God isn't bothered by your repeated petty requests. In fact, He *wants* to give you good things (see Luke 11:11-13). If it's important to you, it's important to your Father. That's how connected He is to you. That's the bond He shares with you. Kind of hard to believe, I admit. And that's another mystery, isn't it? That God would care about the common, everyday, trivial things that affect your life? But He does. He really does. And He wants you to bring to Him anything that threatens to worry you, no matter how unspiritual or secular it may sound (see Phil. 4:6-7; 1 Pet. 5:7).

Prayer is a way to share your entire life with God, not just the "religious bits."

You can't get around this fact: God wants us to ask.

Even so, He does reserve the right to say no to our requests. And that's why we get anxious, because we never know if or when He'll say yes. We only know we're supposed to ask. Apparently, He wants us to talk to Him. After all, that's what friends do. They hang out and talk. And children ask their fathers for things—lots of things—all the time. That's what they are supposed to do. It's a normal part of the unique relationship we have with God.

There's something about seeing His children ask Him for things that pleases Him. What father wouldn't want his children to express their needs and wants to him? If you're a parent, you understand the happiness that fills your heart when your son or daughter depends on you for his or her needs. But just like children, we don't always know what to ask for. We only know what's in front of us at the moment, what we're currently experiencing in life. We only know where it hurts. So we ask our

Father to give us those things that make sense to us. We can't always know if our request is laced with selfishness or if it is God's will. We can't obsess over whether or not we had a bad attitude for 30 seconds on Tuesday of last week. We're not that smart or spiritual.

Don't get me wrong: It's a healthy thing to examine your heart regularly and see if there is anything to confess before God. Think of it as brushing and flossing your soul. But if prayer is to be more of a lifestyle for us and not just an event, we won't always have the time or convenience to pause and reflect before opening a conversation with God. Life comes at us too fast for that.

* * *

I have been a follower of Jesus since I was 16. I have been in ministry for over two decades. I have a seminary degree. I've read books. I've written books. I've heard some of the world's greatest Christian speakers. And in spite of all this, I still don't fully understand prayer. I can understand the discipline of it. I understand what some call the obligation of it. I can quote verses about it. I can recite the acronyms and formulas we've come up with to help us pray. But how it works is still a big mystery to me. I can't tell you why it works sometimes and other times it produces nothing. This frustration is what has many teenagers and young adults questioning the validity and practicality of prayer. There's tension there, I agree. All I know is that prayer is way more than a Christian activity. To me, it's simply an overflow of a relationship with a God who is just as mysterious as prayer is. And I'm okay with that.

So if you're wondering how you should pray, I would suggest that you treat God as if He's walking through life with you 24-7. Talk with Him at any time about anything and everything. If you believe He knows you perfectly and yet loves you unconditionally, there are no taboo subjects in your personal prayers. Find your own comfort zone with prayer. Be like David: brutally honest about every experience, thought and emotion.

I have a son whose motto is "It never hurts to ask." A while back, we were at the mall, and he asked for one of those frozen slushy things.

"Sorry, pal," I said, "I'm all out of cash."

"What if I can get a free sample, Dad? Can I have that?"

"Sure, go for it."

So Davis approached the vendor and asked, "Can I have a sample of your strawberry slushy?"

"We don't give samples, kid," the employee quickly replied.

Davis returned without getting what he wanted, and it didn't seem to bother him. But about 30 minutes later, as we were leaving the mall, he walked up to the same employee, altering his request a little.

"Excuse me, but how much are your free samples?"

"Oh, they're free of course," she replied.

Returning to me and sporting a strawberry-colored mustache and a big grin, Davis announced, "Never hurts to ask, Dad."

There are things in life you really want but may not think you deserve. I hate to tell you this, but you probably never will feel like you deserve them. There are other things that just seem out of your reach, beyond you, too much to ask for. And there are still other things that you feel guilty for bothering God with. And you feel guilty for not praying more or for not giving your church more of your time and money. You hesitate in prayer as you think back over how little you've read your Bible or because you've missed church recently. Or maybe you just think you're too big of a sinner to be asking God for anything other than forgiveness. But do it anyway.

It never hurts to ask.

CHAPTER 6

SLEUTHING FOR THE TRUTH

THE MYSTERY OF THE FAITH

[Hold] to the mystery of the faith.
1 Timothy 3:9, *NASB*

In the early morning hours of June 5, 2002, an intruder broke into the Salt Lake City home of Ed and Lois Smart. All the home's doors had been locked, but the alarm had not been activated that evening, making the intruder's entry undetectable. Silently slithering his way up to their daughters' bedroom, he abducted 14-year-old Elizabeth from her bed, threatening to harm her and her younger sister if either of them made a sound. Too terrified to scream, 9-year-old Mary Katherine hid for over two hours, until just before 4 A.M. when she gathered the courage to tell her parents what had happened.

In a state of shock and disbelief, the Smarts immediately called the police and began notifying family, friends and neighbors. A search launched in the neighborhood came up empty. Later that morning, Ed Smart appeared on television, pleading for the kidnapper to return his daughter. Utilizing every resource available—flyers, the Internet, radio and television—a massive search and manhunt began.

More than 2,000 volunteers meticulously combed the nearby surrounding hills, and the police and even the FBI mobilized their massive resources to recover the innocent preteen; but no one was able to find any clues to her whereabouts or to who the kidnapper was. Nothing. And they couldn't begin to imagine who would do such a thing.

Days turned into weeks, and weeks turned into months. Prayers seemed to fall on deaf ears. Hope waned. Stolen right from under her parent's supervision, Elizabeth seemed to have simply vanished. All that was left of her were photographs and memories.

Drifting Off Course

Something is missing in this generation, something abducted in the night while we were asleep. Something about our faith has failed to resonate with the present age, failed to communicate, failed to connect.

The other night, a 17-year-old boy stood in the doorway of our kitchen and asked, "Jeff, do you ever get bored with Christianity?"

"What do you mean?" I asked, wanting more clarification.

"I mean how Church and Christians are so . . . uninteresting. Every Sunday, it's the same program. The same format. Christians look and act the same. It's like nobody can be themselves. As if there's some rule that says if you think or live outside the box, you're not really a Christian or something."

"Hmm," I said, nodding my head in agreement.

Now you have to know Andrew, an extremely gifted young man. God has given him a creative mind and consequently a disdain for the status quo—he's exactly the kind of person who can make a difference. Unfortunately, his kind are often shunned by the Church, discouraged for wanting to challenge accepted practices or ask the hard questions.

After thinking for a few seconds, I continued, "Yes. I do get bored with the bland, black-and-white faith that is passed off as genuine Christianity. And, bro, that may be why you don't see more people like you and me in the Church today."

Later, I reflected on our conversation and concluded that at the heart of Andrew's dilemma are the questions, What *is* Christianity? How do you define it? What does it look like? And how much of what we see today resembles the original? Is our current Christianity more classic or counterfeit? How far away from the faith have we drifted, if at all? If one of the 12 disciples wandered into the average church next Sunday, would he identify with the faith he finds there?

Maybe. But to many in our culture today, Christianity (i.e., the Church) is dull and uninteresting—even confusing. It bothers people that there are so many different churches that (either subtly or not so subtly) preach their brand of Christianity as the "right one."

But who's right? Which church really has the truth? Which one is doing it like Jesus intended? Which one is truly Christian? Is it the old established church that preaches the Bible verse by verse for 55 minutes on Sundays? Is it the liturgically driven congregation that repeats the same practices and prayers each week, followed by a 10-minute homily? Or is it that new hip postmodern church plant with its coffee, candles and creative media crew? They're all so different. Who's right? Which of these truly speaks for God? And how did we end up where we are today?

A Little History, If You Please

Many years ago, there was a small group of people who followed Jesus. They loved and needed one another very much because they lived during a time when their government wasn't very nice to Christians. In fact, sometimes the government would kidnap some of these believers and turn them into afternoon snacks at the local zoo (popularly known as the Roman Coliseum). Then along came an emperor named Constantine. He became famous for letting the Christians worship more freely. About a hundred years later, the Roman Empire went the way of the dodo.

And yet the Christian faith kept spreading. Leaders in the Church gathered periodically to discuss important doctrinal matters. This was necessary because some false teachers made scurrilous claims, such as that the Old Testament was not really God's Word, that Jesus wasn't fully God, or that Jesus only appeared to be human. These central questions had to be hashed out.

For nearly 1,000 years, there was only one Church. Through a gradual series of events leading up to the year 1054, the one Church divided into two. The eastern (Orthodox) church and the western (Roman Catholic) church disagreed about rituals, politics and doctrines such as how to understand the role of the Holy Spirit and whether the bishop of Rome (as pope) should have authority over all the churches.

Partly in response to the advancement of Muslim armies toward Europe and partly to expand their own borders, the Pope and many of Europe's rulers launched the Crusades during the Middle Ages—which turned out to be a public relations nightmare. Marching to the Holy Land, the Crusaders took Jerusalem in 1099 and promptly massacred the Muslims, Jews and eastern Christians who were there. About 100 years later, the Muslims retook the city and established control over the land. Deep wounds and suspicions from that time have never been healed.

Meanwhile, the Catholic part of Christianity continued to expand its borders, but with power came a growing abuse of authority and position among its leaders. Some priests even started selling forgiveness to parishioners to make more money for the church. Fed up with all this greed and corruption, a German monk in the sixteenth century named Martin said enough is enough and started a spiritual revolution. He protested against the Catholic Church and its abuses. Those who followed agreed with him, and his example became known as Protestants (because they were protesting, get it?).

Eventually, these Protestants broke away from the Catholic Church, forming even further distinctions between themselves: Lutherans, Calvinists, French Huguenots and the Church of England, among others. Many of the English who settled in the New World were Christians seeking religious freedom. This led to even more flavors of Christianity in the Colonies, such as Puritans, Congregationalists, Presbyterians, Baptists, Quakers, Methodists and Episcopalians.

Fast-forward to the 1900s. By this time, three presidents had been shot, most homes enjoyed indoor plumbing, and the famous tent revival had been invented. People by the hundreds came to Jesus at these meetings. But there were challenges on the horizon as well. Modern thought, combined with a growing dependence on science, led many to conclude that the old-time religion of Christianity was really nothing more than a fairy tale for grown-ups. Then came two World Wars and the Great Depression, and suddenly we needed God again. Despite modernism, we were, by and large, a nation of churchgoers with society pretty much agreeing on most basic moral issues. Then Billy Graham reinvented the tent revival in the 1950s, drawing tens of thousands to the altar. And preachers never spoke the same way again.

The 1960s brought another revolution—a cultural one this time—changing everything from fashion to the family, from music to movies, from civil rights to sexual expression. And another president was shot. Some older folks wondered if this was the end of Western civilization, and many still blame the turmoil of the '60s on Elvis and his gyrating pelvis.

The younger generation, for the most part, viewed church as archaic and irrelevant. It was time once again for a revolution—a revolution within a revolution. People began finding Jesus outside the official church in places like campus and parachurch organizations, even in communes. Mainline denominations began to see drastic declines in attendance, and in the 1980s nondenominational Bible churches started springing up.

Before long, a conservative movement arose, but many within it became more interested in political power and moral issues than they were in helping people find Jesus. The children of that generation grew tired of being preached at, but because they still wanted to know God, they again began looking for Him outside the established church. Today, tens of thousands of people, many of them older, are coming together to form new communities of faith. Sometimes these groups are called churches. Other times they prefer to be known as "faith communities" or "faith gatherings."

What Have We Become?

Admittedly, that history of the Church may be a gross oversimplification, but if we look back to the first-century group of believers, we see that we've drifted off course, away from God's original idea. We've become a culture of mega-church-worshiping, entertainment-minded, multimillion-dollar, consumer-driven superstores. And even those churches that are still small want to get big so that they can play with the big boys. But is that the vision we're supposed to sell to a generation living in a world of hunger, disease, poverty, addiction and an increasing frustration with organized religion?

How did we get from being one Church to so many off-shoots, denominations, sects and brands? Why so many divisions in the Christian faith? Scholars estimate that there are more than 2,600 groups today who claim to corner the market on what it means to be "the Church." From 1 to 2,600!

Are all these divisions necessarily wrong? Personally I don't think so, as long as we are willing to work together toward a common cause. And as long as we can join hands as brothers and sisters in a shared faith—regardless of race, social standing or political views.

In reality, most churches have their own personality and style. Their doctrine may be mainstream Christianity, but they are unique in their look, feel, practices and traditions. I'm okay with that. In fact, I think it's healthy. Different people enjoy varying styles and strategies for worship, teaching, ministry and reaching our world. Once you cover the basics of the faith, churches (like individual Christians) ought to be able to freely express themselves in ways that best reflect their personalities, interests and local culture. That's why a church (or a Christian) in Uganda should look different from her American counterpart. And even within the same country, there are subcultures, people groups, tribes where certain cultural values are particularly important, whether it be art, music, the environment or social justice. That's simply celebrating who God made us uniquely to be. It's a way we can bring a one-of-a-kind offering to the Church, community and world: many churches, one common heartbeat. It's the same lyric of Christianity, sung with different instruments playing different types of music.

How liberating is it that you don't have to look, talk, act or even worship like other Christians! If you trust in Jesus, *you're in*. That's it. Period. But to feel out of place in a church because you don't measure up somehow or because you didn't bring a Bible or dress the right way . . . well, that's not cool.

And that's not vintage Christianity.

What Makes Us Christian?

Unfortunately, the perception that is sometimes broadcast today is that only those who are like us will get into heaven. To some, Christendom is like an exclusive club. And clubs have members. You can join if you want, but you'll have to pay your weekly dues.

Our unbelieving friends wonder, *If Christianity is one faith, then why is there so much division and bickering within the Christian community?* It puzzles them why some evangelical churches seem to be religious clubs for the intolerant, the self-righteous and the closed-minded. They wonder if there's any room for devoted Christians who don't share the same political affiliations as most conservative believers. They want to know if they have to believe everything we believe. And if not, how can we claim to embrace one faith?

Have you ever seen those cheesy church signs that include everything they believe in their name, like *The First Free-Will, Premillennial, Baptistic, Full Immersion, Full-Gospel Church of God's Holy Word in Christ Jesus Our Lord, Amen*? The underlying message is, if you don't believe like us, you probably shouldn't come. What happened that our personal preferences are sometimes made into official doctrine?

I once heard a preacher give a sermon about television. He called it the "idiot box" and said that anyone who watched it had "square eyes." Then he called on the congregation to unplug their television sets and put them in the closet. He boasted about the fact that his family only received three channels on their TV, thus preventing the evils of cable from entering the sanctity of their home. Looking around the huge auditorium that morning, I noted that some faces wore a look of surprised disbelief while others heartily nodded with righteous "Amens." As I continued scanning the room, I also noticed two men manning television cameras (I guess TV is evil but Christian TV is okay). Following that sermon, I went home, made a sandwich and watched an old Tarzan movie on the idiot box.

Once I received a phone call from a very upset parent. He was disturbed because I was taking our teenagers out for pizza on Wednesdays to a restaurant that served alcohol. I assured him I wasn't ordering pitchers of beer for the kids and that we pretty much filled the entire restaurant with our group. Besides, it wasn't as if we were bellying up to a smoke-filled bar. We were at a mainstream family restaurant. Unphased by my eloquent defense, the parent informed me that if I continued taking students there, his daughter would not be allowed to go. I asked him if he had any alternative ideas about where we might go instead. His suggestion was that we take our students to the cafeteria of the local hospital. He said it was a clean, family-friendly environment and the food was healthy. I think that's when the phone went dead.

Another church I know of sponsors a father-daughter banquet each year. It's a time for girls to bond with their dads. Great idea, right? But here's the deal: Prior to coming to the banquet, the girls are required to submit their dresses for approval by someone on the church staff to ensure the hemline isn't too high or the neckline too low. Funny . . . I thought a girl's dad would be the best judge of his daughter's modesty.

Extreme examples? Possibly. But has our faith been reduced to issues of entertainment, alcohol and fashion? Is that all we have to offer?

Christianity has a reputation in your city, and it's based on the Church's reputation in your city. How is the Church perceived in your town? What kind of name is it making for Jesus? How is it doing? What do people think of it?

Maybe they would jump at the chance to criticize or condemn the Church. Or it's possible they have little or no opinion, due to our minimal contact with them. In that case, for them the faith can be a real mystery (and not in a good way).

Suppose a college student from a European country (let's call him Ian) comes to live with you for a year. And suppose Ian has no particular religious preference, though he is familiar with the world's major faiths. Imagine, while enjoying coffee and a slice of pie one day at your neighborhood bistro, the following conversation occurs:

Ian: So tell me about your faith.

You: Sure. What would you like to know?

Ian: What would you like to tell?

You: Well, to begin with, we believe in God.

Ian: Like the Jews?

You: Yes, but with a slightly different twist.

Ian: Okay, go on.

You: We follow Jesus and His teachings. He had a lot to say about how we should live.

Ian: You mean like doing the *right* thing instead of the *wrong* thing . . . having high moral standards and all that?

You: Right.

Ian: Like the Mormons. I've heard they have very strict moral codes about dress, food and beverage consumption, and premarital sex. They don't even drink coffee because they consider it a drug.

You: Well, yes, but . . . we're not quite that strict. We like some drugs . . . I mean *drinks*.

Ian: (*Laughing*) I'm with you, brother. And do you pray to your God?

You: Absolutely. Prayer is a huge part of our faith.

Ian: Really? My Muslim friend pauses to pray five times every day. So your faith is like Islam then?

You: Oh, no. We're totally different from that. You see—

Ian: What about a sacred book? The Hindus have the Vedas and the Muslims their Koran.

You: And we have the Bible—God's Word.

Ian: What about meditation?

You: Right, we meditate on the truths we believe.

Ian: Most Eastern religions do that. What about personal responsibility? Does your faith teach that you get what you give? Or the idea that your actions carry spiritual consequences?

You: Absolutely. The Bible clearly says that a man reaps what he sows—

Ian: Just like karma.

You: Well, no . . . I mean . . . kind of, uh . . . but different.

Ian: And your founder is Jesus, whom you believe to be a God-Man, both human and divine?

You: Right. The Son of God.

Ian: I see. Like Krishna. Is it possible your Jesus and Krishna could be the same person, one maybe a reincarnation of the other?

You: No! No! Jesus is . . . well . . . He's the Son of God . . . He's just Jesus. The One of a kind. Original. The *only One.*

Ian: But those who follow Krishna believe he lived hundreds of years before your Christ.

You: I don't know anything about that.

Ian: Sorry to break the news to you, man, but it seems to me that your religion bears a fundamental similarity to all the other major faiths in the world. Isn't that because they all basically worship the same God but with different traditions and approaches?

You: Oh, not at all. You couldn't be more wrong. Christianity stands alone—separate from all the others because we worship Jesus who rose from the dead. No other religious leader has done that.

Ian: But if He's alive, then where is He?

You: Oh. Umm, well, He had to go back to heaven and build mansions. But He'll be back someday to take us home.

Ian: How convenient. Let me ask you one more question. If Christianity is, as you say, the one and only true way to God, then why does it produce so many splinter cells? Why so many different kinds of churches and denominations, many who strongly oppose the teachings of the others? I hear one Christian define Christianity one way, and someone from another church defines it very differently. One told me that I would have to give up drinking if I chose your faith, but someone else told me that that wasn't important and even bought me a drink! I thought you Christians all believed the same, but now I'm confused. Your faith seems to have broken into camps with each one redefining the faith in a way that best suits your own personalities and peculiar moral views. So my question is, If your God is so great and powerful, then why can't He persuade His own followers to agree?

You: Well, because people are just dumb, and they don't always listen to the one *true truth*.

Ian: And whose truth would that be? Yours?

You: Is that your cell phone? Oh, then it must be mine. Let me take this call. Check, please!

Can you see how our faith can be about as clear as mud to the average person who doesn't embrace it? But the unchurched are not the only ones who see inconsistency.

A Fish Story

Those of us in the Church also see discrepancies when today's Christianity is compared to its first-century ancestor. Unlike today, the Early Church didn't enjoy volumes of doctrinal teaching but clung to a few foundation stones that made up their belief system. Long before Jesus' followers carried Bibles, attended seminaries, wore Christian T-shirts or bracelets, or adorned their cars with bumper stickers, they were forced to communicate their faith through their words, lifestyles and relationships.

Then some creative Christian came up with an ingenious idea. This person noticed that the Greek word *ichthus* (meaning "fish") could serve as an acrostic for *Iesous Christos Theou Uios Soter*, or "Jesus Christ God's Son Savior." The story goes that upon greeting each other, one person would draw a half-circle in the dirt, and if the other person was a follower of Jesus, he or she would draw a corresponding half-circle, thus completing the traditional icon of a fish. Whether or not they actually did that is debatable. But one thing is clear.

This fish logo fit the faith well, and it stuck. After all, Jesus fed 5,000 with a few fish and loaves of bread. He also told His disciples He would make them into "fishers of men" (Matt. 4:19; Mark 1:17). Water baptism evoked similar images of fish in water. Tertullian, a second-century theologian, put it this way: "We, little fishes, after the image of our *Ichthys*, Jesus Christ, are born in the water."

For centuries, this fish symbol has been used to represent the essence of Christianity. You've probably seen it on a shirt or the back of a car, in which case you may have also seen the Darwin symbol—a fish with legs. *How dare they! The fish symbol is ours alone, right?* Not exactly. The Greeks and Romans, along with many other pagans, used the fish symbol in their religions long before Christianity got hold of it—but the pagans used it in sexually explicit ways.

Like other cultural icons throughout history, the fish was adopted (and redeemed) by Christians to be used as one of our symbols—this one a symbol for God. But hey, it was already recognizable in the culture, and it worked. (We did the same thing with the cross, transforming it from merely a symbol of death into an eternal icon of love. We are still the only faith whose primary "logo" is an instrument of brutal execution. Can you imagine how morbid it would be for a company to use a hangman's noose or an electric chair as their trademark? Christianity, revolutionary by nature, took the cross and reinvented it.)

And here's why the fish was such a perfect way to identify and bond believers to one another: It said a lot about the faith with just a few words.

- *Jesus Christ*—the prophesied anointed One, the long-awaited Messiah

- *God's Son*—the eternal One, fully divine, God become flesh to identify with us

- *Savior*—restoring a sinful and undeserving humanity from sin's slavery and penalty

132

The fish was the Nike swoosh of first-century Christianity. Without uttering a sound, one symbol said it all. Imagine this symbol in the context of the Early Church, composed not of millions of faithful, but of small, scattered, close-knit communities of faith. The early followers of Jesus lived in a hostile Roman climate and knew that at any moment, they or their fellow believers could be called on to renounce their faith in the Messiah and instead declare allegiance to Caesar as lord. And if they refused to change, they were routinely beaten or tortured or fed to lions—or all of the above.

If the world you lived in constantly threatened you because you believed in Jesus, you'd be very motivated to gather in a house full of other people who shared the same basic faith. When you and 30 other Christians were rounded up and led to a painful death, it wouldn't matter what race the other Christians were, or whether they were slave or free, or whether they disagreed with you about local politics—or even whether they disagreed about Caesar being the Beast from Revelation 11!

Even major differences were put aside in light of the tough circumstances. In that moment, only one thing mattered—your one common creed: a shared faith in Jesus Christ, God's Son, Savior. That was the banner cry of the Early Christians, their unifying hope, and it gave them strength to endure martyrs' deaths. Because of their united faith in the midst of persecution, in Tertullian's words, "the blood of the martyrs became the seed of the church." This common simple faith allowed them to look past the things that threatened to divide them.

Maybe what we need today is some good old-fashioned persecution. Not persecution because of some high moral

Chapter 6

standard, as honorable as that is. Instead, maybe we need to be rounded up simply because we remind people of Jesus—the One who healed, helped and loved. But it's not that simple today, is it?

For an organization whose primary mission is to be known for its fervent love (see John 13:35), there sure is a lot of division, disagreement, arguing, fighting and splitting within and among churches. We don't fight over whether Jesus is Savior. We have bigger fish to fry: things like which translation of the Bible is best, who gets to use the church van and why royal blue *must* be the color of the sanctuary's new carpet. And when the disagreement gets nasty enough, we pick up our toys and go play down the street at another house of worship.

Unfortunately, splitting a church has been a common way to plant a new one. Often it comes down to a power struggle between two opposing personalities—usually the old guard (who feel it's their responsibility to protect the church from new ideas) against someone (anyone) with a more progressive approach. Throw in some type-A personalities, a few control freaks and some big tithers (often the same people) and you've got yourself a caged death match. Then come the special prayer gatherings (secret ones at first) that soon spill over into church-wide town-hall meetings. That's when the gloves come off and things get real ugly. Before long, it's escalated into a full-scale war. Hurtful (sometimes hateful) words are spoken. Voices are raised. Scriptures are confidently quoted by both sides. At times a punch or two is thrown. There have even been death threats.

Church attendance may actually spike during these times because people love to see a good fight. It may be the first time in years some people pay close attention in church! But then the dissenting group threatens to leave, taking people with them. Usually those words signal the beginning of the ground campaign in this war. Taking people away means taking away the money they deposit in the offering plate each Sunday. People may storm out of the room, or they may stay and debate who's going to get the building (and the debt). Then the split officially happens, though what is publicly announced is that the Lord is leading some of the brothers and sisters to a new calling.

The two sides go their respective ways, each believing they're right and the other is wrong.

Depending on the size and community presence of the church, the local newspaper carries the story. Now everybody knows, including those who have always used this kind of inconsistency as their official excuse for not being interested in Christianity. Like a nasty celebrity divorce, the church split becomes lunchtime gossip and the butt of local jokes. And people shake their heads with prophetic pride, saying, "See, I told you those Christians were a bunch of phonies. They're always trying to straighten out everybody else and tell us how bad we are, when they can't even take care of themselves."

It's just as sad when churches of different denominations and traditions fail to work together for a common cause. Or worse, when nondenominational churches criticize denominational churches that aren't like them.

It's not that Christians should never disagree on matters of faith and practice. A healthy debate can be a refining and purifying exercise for the Christian Church. That process is part of the way we've arrived at our current understanding of many critical areas of faith. But it's confusing to a watching world, and it's a stumbling block to them.

It's a sign of the beginning of the end, and evidence that the fish is beached.

One Way

In the early days, the Christian faith didn't have an official name. Some called it "the Way" (Acts 9:2; 19:9; 22:4; 24:14,22), likely derived from Jesus' words recorded in John 14:6. Although some considered it a passing religious fad, a flash-in-the-pan revolution like all the others that preceded it, most considered Christianity some sort of Jewish sect (Acts 24:5,14; 28:22), while some Jews viewed the group loyal to the dead, charismatic rabbi as a cult.

So what exactly is "the faith"? Is *American* Christianity what Jesus had in mind while hanging on that cross? Does being a part of a faith community mean merely adopting a detailed, fixed set of values and beliefs, or is there more to it than that? What's the difference between *unity* and *uniformity*? Is being right our ultimate goal?

At the core of Christian faith is the Person of Jesus. Everything flows from this. *Everything.* This is in no way a devaluation of doctrine, theology, teaching or catechism. I've spent over two decades passionately communicating truth to people. I still do. A master of theology degree hangs in my study, and I worked hard for that piece of paper. I would never call for us to ignore or downplay classic Christian beliefs—quite the opposite: Our connection to historical Christian beliefs is a critical lifeline, keeping us grounded, stable and centered. We can never exchange truth for experience or expedience.

But in our sincere efforts to make sense of our faith and get it right, we have systematized, organized and Americanized "the faith that was once for all entrusted to the saints" (Jude 3). As a result, we've robbed that faith of its mysticism and mystery. And when the mystery is gone, it becomes a rerun: predictable, unimpressive, something we only embrace for sentimental value or to feel good.

This neatly packaged religion is what we market to our unbelieving communities and to the next generation in our churches. But they've seen it all before. And they're not buying it now. They are unimpressed with a faith that has no mystery, no loose ends, no unanswered questions, no unknowns. To them, Christianity is, on one hand, complex and full of corporate religious duties. But on the other hand, it is so uninspiring that it can be summed up in a few phrases: "Get saved." "Live right." "Give up stuff." "Give your money." "Bring others into the building."

That's the "abundant life" we're offering to our world. Anybody want some?

The beauty of our faith is veiled to a world that so desperately needs it.

If we should feel obligated to do anything, it should be to return to the potent faith that once shook the world, before it went from organic to corporate. When we strip away all the makeup and decorations; when we remove the cultural extras, even our secondary moral customs; when we peel back the layers of Christendom, looking past television preachers, Christian music and publishing, beyond the name on the church sign; when we go past the rules, taboos, duties and spiritual disciplines;

when we get to the essence of Christianity, what do we find? What's there that's worth giving away our time and life energy for, that's worth giving our blood for?

There's got to be something better than a cheesy slogan. Something more than a trendy presentation. Something more substantive than an hour on Sunday or salivating over the next mega-church fad or the latest Barna research results. There has to be something better to do than to argue about whether to preach topically (like Jesus) or verse by verse.

So what makes us "Christian"? Just ask the first people known by that name. Without laptops or Microsoft Word, they wrote a story that rocked human history.

Without multimillion-dollar buildings, sound systems, electric guitars or seminary-trained pastors, they built the Church from nothing. Without billboards or websites, they launched a worldwide advertising campaign for their Cause. They *were* the Internet.

They had no church programs, but what they had was immeasurably better. And more effective. They had the Person of Jesus, and their loyal belief in Him captured their souls and changed their lives down to the roots.

Profoundly simple, isn't it?

But though it's simple, it is also one of the deepest "truth wells" we'll ever draw from. Being Christian doesn't mean all our questions are answered, but that didn't seem to matter to those early believers. They didn't know where this vision would take them. Their great risk was overshadowed by faith—faith in Jesus.

What makes us "Christian"? *Christians are people who embrace Jesus in their spirit.*

Things have a tendency to come full circle. What goes around usually does come around. It's true in music, fashion, art, advertising and architecture. I believe it will be true of the Christian faith as well. Not that all churches will become unified, but that there will be an awakening among God's people. And maybe we'll rediscover what's really important about our Christianity. I anticipate that more big churches will shrink and die as new ones are born, some even reborn to a new purpose—a better one this time. I see a reawakening among churches and a return to our roots—to vintage Christianity: a return to the Way, to a faith that is raw, untamed and pure. A faith that "once was lost, but now is found."

* * *

On March 12, 2003, nine months after Elizabeth Smart's predawn abduction, a long-haired, disheveled-looking man was spotted on the street not too far from the Smart's home. Accompanying him were two women wearing veils. The man turned out to be a self-proclaimed vagabond minister named Brian David Mitchell (who called himself Emmanuel David Isaiah). His two traveling companions turned out not to be two women, but a woman and a girl—Elizabeth Smart—hidden under a wig, sunglasses and veil. Mitchell and his accomplice were arrested and taken into custody. And Elizabeth finally got to go home to her family. For nine months she had been closer than anyone could have imagined, held captive in several makeshift camps hidden in the woods of a nearby canyon. Hidden almost in plain sight.

Jesus' disciples worldwide are waking up to the fact that the mystery of our common, beautiful faith has been near us all along. Like an ancient artifact, it's been disguised under a thick veil of tradition and human-centered Christianity. Right under our noses.

In a world that is growing progressively hostile toward Christians and with the possibility of an end-times persecution, it won't matter what kind of Christian you are.

It will only matter that you like fish.

CHAPTER 7

DECIPHERING THE ANCIENT CODE

THE MYSTERY OF THE BIBLE

Your word, O LORD, is eternal.

Psalm 119:89

I speak at a lot of churches, schools, conferences and retreats. I get to hang out with people of various backgrounds and of all ages—teenagers, college students, single adults and parents of teenagers, among others. They're all different, but if they were all in one place together, most of them would admit that the Bible is not a very important part of their lives. It's not because they don't believe in it. They do. And it's not because they don't think it should be important. They do. Back in the day, most homes had a family Bible, a huge book big enough to choke a mule. In it were housed the family archives (records of marriages, births, deaths, and other important events), but mainly it was just decoration.

Many people today have their own personal copy of the Bible. Some may carry it to school, work and even church, but many Bibles stay at home, resting comfortably on bedside tables, shelves and desktops. And why? Because the Bible is intimidating.

Unfortunately, most people feel that looking inside a Bible would be like looking inside a computer: It's complicated, confusing and encoded; it contains undecipherable language, hidden features and mystifying messages. In a word, intimidating.

As such, the chance of most people cracking open the Good Book is about as likely as them scaling Mount McKinley. To these sincere people, the Bible is a book of confusing and ancient stories about judgments and wars, obscure kings, miracles and the Messiah. But what does it actually mean to them? Not much, really.

But this isn't to say they're unfamiliar with the Bible itself. They might throw out a few well-worn names like Moses or

Samson or pull out a famous quote like "love thy neighbor" or an occasional "the Lord is my shepherd." But to many, the Bible is simply a collection of stories that by this time have taken on near-mythical status. The characters lived too long ago and too far away. They had weird names too, like Artaxerxes, Sennacherib and Zerubbabel. (Who names their kid Zerubbabel?) It makes it hard to identify with those people. Actually, we feel we have virtually nothing in common with them. Even for faithful churchgoers, the Bible can be more of a prop than a personal user's manual for life. Not true for everyone, mind you. Just for most.

Hand a copy of the Bible to the average churchgoer and ask him or her to explain it, and you'll likely get that deer-in-the-headlights stare. Sure, we've made great strides in translating the Bible and marketing it to consumers. The Western world is flooded with study Bibles, study methods, how-to books, steps, charts and diagrams. There's a multimillion-dollar industry committed to getting the Word of God in the hands of the people, and rightly so. But in spite of this noble, Herculean effort, the Bible remains largely a sealed and secret document to most. A closed book, figuratively and literally—an ancient code.

Perceived Troubles

To crack this code, we have to begin by making certain concessions. We have to acknowledge our lack of knowledge, admitting there's mystery in the Book. We also have to confess our limitations and hang-ups about the Bible. We have to revisit the Scriptures, remixing a fresh perspective in the process. It's important that as we do this, we remain honest with ourselves.

There's no one to impress here and no one to judge us for our authenticity.

We have to admit that there are things about the Bible that trouble us. Stuff that really bothers us. Things that make us hesitate even picking it up. We wonder why, since we're Christians, God didn't make the Bible more self-explanatory. Like, why don't we automatically get it? I mean, God wrote it, right? And He wrote it for us. And we're His children, and He wants us to understand His Word, right? So why is it that a PDA or an iPod is easier to understand than the Bible? Why isn't the Bible more user-friendly? Why does the Bible seems so threatening, so unapproachable?

For one thing, the average Bible is thick, and that's intimidating to those who don't list "reading" in their top-five favorite hobbies. Most people's reading habits include magazines and Web pages, so to even think about tackling a book that covers thousands of years of human history seems—shall we say— daunting. Then, if you muster the nerve to open up the Bible, you discover the pages are, well . . . paper-thin. You find yourself licking your fingers to turn only one page at a time. Still, you unintentionally tear a page and that upsets you, maybe even making you feel like you've committed a small sin. And the print is usually so small that only Lilliputians can read it.

Then you discover the Bible isn't composed like other books. You're accustomed to reading books that are arranged in sequential order, the way a story is usually told. But in the Bible, the story line doesn't always follow along sequentially. Though it does eventually tell one big story, books like Psalms talk about events and circumstances that occurred several books earlier.

One book found midway through the Old Testament tells the story of someone who most likely lived during the time of Genesis (see Job). In addition, some books appear to have no relation to the one that precedes or follows it, making the Bible seem disjointed, unorganized and random. Other books repeat the same stories as the one before it, causing you to wonder, *Why all the redundancy?* (See, for example, the books of 1 and 2 Kings, 1 and 2 Chronicles and the Gospels.) This can be confusing to the average reader.

Another obstacle people have regarding the Bible is that though it was originally written centuries ago, we're expected to read it as if it had been written this morning. In reality, the Bible (and all its parts) was written to a people with whom we feel we have very little in common. We don't think the way they did or practice any of their customs. *Hello!* They lived thousands of years ago! That in itself creates quite a gap between us. They also spoke a different language, one that's not usually offered in our high schools or even our universities. Theirs was a different country, a different culture and a worldview poles apart from our own, and because we identify best with those who are most like us, getting into the world of the Bible becomes a huge challenge. After all, as a general rule, we don't go to Turkish movies or read Russian periodicals, so immersing ourselves in ancient Near Eastern biblical culture for 30 minutes a day is a stretch for many twenty-first-century Westerners.

Another thing that adds mystery to the Bible is that it's only been accessible to common people for just over 500 years. For the first 1,400 years, only those who were highly educated (or super rich) had personal access to it.

A related trouble is that sometimes even today (perhaps unintentionally), the Bible is presented as a book only understood by professionals, as if there's an unwritten law that says the preacher preaches the Word, and you could never understand it on your own. After all, the preacher is the shepherd, and you're just a sheep, a fact reinforced all the more when he or she highlights the hidden meaning of some Hebrew or Greek word.

It's always been a danger in the Church for scholars to hijack the Bible and use knowledge as a weapon to hold common people hostage. In reality, such power-hungry people simply want a way to keep you under their authority. Be very wary of ministers or preachers who make the Bible seem like an ancient document that only *they* can decipher. After all, if you started understanding the Bible for yourself, then what control would they have over you? Keep in mind: I *am* a pastor, called to a ministry of equipping and encouragement. But I don't hold exclusive rights to the truth. That privilege is available to any God seeker.

Granted, the pastor typically has some theological education, experience and competence the average audience member doesn't. But we have to be careful not to fall into the abyss of the clergy-laity gap.

Some of my friends struggle with the Bible because it's been used to justify oppression of women, racial prejudice, religious bigotry, and even war.

If that's not enough to deter you, the Bible is the only book on your shelf you feel guilty for not reading every day. (By the way, what have you spent more time doing today—reading your Bible or reading your email? See what I mean?) Honestly, none of us has been consistent in that discipline of daily Bible reading, have we? So we end up stalling somewhere near the intersection of Feeling Guilty and Trying Harder.

Adding to our troubles and the Book's mystery is why it suddenly stopped being written about 2,000 years ago. Hasn't God had anything new, noteworthy or important to say to His people or humanity since then? Haven't there been any more interesting personalities through whose lives we might be encouraged or inspired? If the Bible is living and alive, why does it seem so dead and outdated to some people? And if God wrote the Bible today, would He use Hebrew poetry and first-century teaching methods, or would He write it in a style more suited to our current culture and take into account our various ways of learning? Would His writing mimic *USA Today* or *People* magazine? Would God put His Word on a CD, a DVD or even a blog?

Those are just some of the troubling thoughts and questions that pop into the heads of honest, thinking people. And it's because of these perceived troubles with the Bible that many copies continue to gather dust or become portable filing cabinets for old church bulletins.

The Real Story

So what are we to make of all this? Should we pack our bags and head off to seminary to be professionally trained? Should we pick up a book outlining the latest fad in Bible study methods? Or better yet, buy the DVD series? Maybe sign up for an additional equipping class at church? Perhaps.

Exactly how do you relate to such an old book in today's world? Maybe your reluctance comes as a result of years enduring boring sermons, lectures and Sunday School lessons. If so, know that you're in good company. For years my sons created elaborate Origami sculptures out of offering envelopes while the pastor spoke to the adults for 55 minutes. I'm happy to report there was no permanent damage, and that my boys still love God and think He's interesting. They have, however, requested that I never refer to my messages as "sermons."

Maybe you were dragged (or *drugged!*) to church week after week to hear God's Word preached. But as much as you'd like to enjoy it, you instead find the Bible largely irrelevant and uninteresting. If that's your experience, then allow me to reassure you that the book God wrote, the Bible, is the most exciting, energizing, captivating and creative collection of stories and truth the world has ever seen—the most fascinating document of all time.

More awe-inspiring than surveying the panorama of a Colorado mountaintop just prior to tipping your skis southbound for another run. More adventurous than an action-packed episode of your favorite TV series. More romantic than a classic Hollywood film. More barbaric than *Braveheart*. More emotional than *Saving Private Ryan*. More inspirational than *The Shawshank Redemption*. More suspenseful than an M. Knight Shyamalan thriller. (Okay, those are all guy movies, but what'd you expect?)

I'm here to tell you that the Bible is better than the brochure and hugely underrated—mostly because it's so misunderstood.

Perhaps because of our deep reverence for it as a holy book, we've missed the inspirational earthiness of it—a camera angle of Scripture God intended us to see all along. Is it possible that the way the Bible has been presented to us all these years—as a heavenly textbook to be studied and tested on—has skewed our perception of it, altering our ability to embrace it? For example, Jesus had an unconventional way of communicating God's truth: not by preaching well-oiled, alliterated or acrostic sermons, but by telling stories, illustrating life from God's truth and illustrating God's truth from life (see Matt. 13:34; Mark 4:30,33-34).

He apparently believed God's Word was interesting enough to be translated into common language. Jesus' methods of teaching were fascinating, captivating. He taught with authority, without hammering His sheep with the Word (the goats were another story) (see Matt. 7:29). As He spoke God's Word, "the crowds were amazed" (Matt. 7:28), not because He entertained their minds (though He was entertaining), but because He incorporated God's truth into real life. What a contrast to the rote teaching of the Pharisees and their paint-by-number faith!

It doesn't make sense to me that the One who is this interesting would write a dull, dry, mind-numbing book. And the good news is that He didn't.

So now you're thinking, *Here come the five secrets or seven keys to unlocking the mystery of the Bible.*

Nope.

I promise not to resurrect my seminary classroom notes and bore you with a step-by-step, foolproof method for cracking those hard-to-understand passages of Scripture. Though undoubtedly helpful, all man-made Bible study methods have their limitations. And I'm not about to fool you into thinking that if you simply apply some special formula, you'll figure it out. I can't fully explain to you how all of the Bible is relevant, though I wholeheartedly believe it is. I'm still not exactly sure what Pharaoh or Sennacherib has to do with me, my family, my friends or my world. I don't know how those censuses in the book of Numbers (see chapters 1 and 26) rate on the same level as Jesus' saying, "I am the way and the truth and the life" (John 14:6). Some verses, passages and stories seem more like decoration or background material than life-changing truth. But isn't that the way any great story is written, with main characters, supporting cast members and background material?

I encourage you to read books to discover how the Bible came together and why we believe it to be accurate and reliable. Throw in some Bible study books too if you like. Treat yourself to a well-rounded approach to the Bible. Just remember, there is only one authoritative Book. The rest are written by a bunch of sincere but flawed followers like me who are just trying to help.

The Dynamic Duo

With all its mystery, I think the Bible, even most of the deep parts, can be understood by the average person. So you and I can get it too, provided we're willing to make a little investment. Admittedly, some things that are described in the Bible— like the big miracles—are a bit hard to swallow at first.

But think about how awesome our infinite God must be, and suddenly you have no problem imagining Him performing some mind-bending feat. Still, if you're like me, you wish God would do some world-famous, epic miracle, just to let us know He's still involved in the game. Haven't you secretly wished He would do some modern marvel and astound your unbelieving friends? Like part a river, send fire from heaven or open up the ground and swallow your boss? *Anything* to show us mortals that it's really not about us.

Of course, it's not that He doesn't do the miraculous—it's just that the everyday miracles we see don't quite measure up to those larger-than-life, fall-on-your-face kind of phenomena. God's miracles *are* all around us, but maybe we're not looking at them hard enough or in the right way. Maybe there's more miracle in the unceasing heartbeat in your chest than in God moving a mountain. Perhaps there's more of the supernatural in a reconciled relationship than in walking on water. Could it be that the spiritual, relational and emotional miracles He does today more than outweigh the mere suspension of nature's laws He did in the past?

Possibly.

It's all in the Bible, and part of this mystery is that it does not tell us everything we want to know. Granted, there's tension here, but like any good mystery writer, God doesn't wrap up every story with a neat bow. He doesn't resolve everything at the end of the book like a *Leave It to Beaver* episode. God is more like a writer for *Lost* or *24*, leaving His readers hanging from time to time.

But if the Bible is God's written expression of Himself to mankind (Jesus being the living, human equivalent), exactly how did it happen? More specifically, if God wrote the epistle to the Galatians, why did Paul sign his name to it?

We refer to the Bible as *God's* Word, but human authors actually picked up quills to write it. Furthermore, God apparently chose not to bypass each person's personality, writing style, giftedness or human experience. Many times the story is about the author himself (for example, see 1 Cor. 2–4). This individuality is what makes Psalms read different than Romans. It's why Doctor Luke (of the books of Luke and Acts fame) has a style all his own, which is different from Peter's.

In reality, God partnered with people, weaving His story with His creation's. He formed a marriage between truth and humanity to bring us His written revelation. Amazingly, He chose not to dictate His words to human writers but to gently and invisibly guide the Scripture's authors toward perfection. He supernaturally oversaw their works, making sure we got everything that was in His heart at the time. And as usual, God dipped the author's pens into Earth's culture, drawing from it words, phrases and customs that would have been familiar to the hearers (and ultimately the readers) of Scripture. In doing this, God shows us that even the most mundane things can be used for His purposes.

So when you read Matthew, you're reading *Matthew*. The former tax collector didn't fall into some zombie-like trance when he wrote the first book of the New Testament. Instead, through a union of human memory and a mystical infusion of the Holy Spirit, he recalled with crystalline clarity the words, events, names, places and experiences related to the life and times of Jesus, the Messiah. It was the same for John, Luke and Mark (though Mark had some additional help from Peter, and Luke interviewed many eyewitnesses).

The bottom line? God wanted to tell us something about Himself, mankind, eternity, life and love, so He used people to help Him. The result? The Word of God.

And yes, it does require a certain degree of faith to believe that. Though not a blind faith.

Of course, it might come as a minor disappointment to some people that their Bible wasn't written with the actual "finger of God" as were the Ten Commandments (see Exod. 31:18). But see the genius in the Lord's decision to do it this way instead. Were it not for Him employing human authors, we would not have the books of Psalms or Ecclesiastes, books that identify with the human condition—doubt, struggle, desperation, sin, salvation and forgiveness flow from these masterpieces. God knew what He was doing when He decided His divine Book would largely contain stories about humanity—stories of hope, redemption, grace, conflict and reconciliation—stories about *us*.

God knew it would be impossible for us to identify with perfection and deity, but we could make a soul connection with fellow humans. And that's why it's so unfair to refer to Bible characters as "saints," as if they attained some level of spirituality unavailable to us today. On the contrary, God presents them as they really were: simple dirt-dwellers struggling to follow Yahweh in the context of their own world—and often failing in the process.

Understanding this makes the Bible as a whole start to come alive to us. It becomes a GPS for our souls, helping us navigate even the back roads of life. And that's the way God designed it. He intended for us to bond with biblical characters, to see in them our own sin, struggle, process, faith, obedience and victory.

But what about those issues and areas of life about which the Bible says nothing specific? What are you to do when you face a situation not directly addressed in the written Word? For example, you're trying to choose a college (or a mate!) and several options seem viable to you. Which one should you choose? What does God want you to do? What does the Bible say about picking a college or choosing a spouse or retiring or moving to a different state?

Answer? Nothing. Nada. Zilch. Zero.

So if you're trying to decide where to go to college, stop looking for the passage that says:

> And when thou shalt come to a place in life when thine education shall cost thee many *denarii*, thou shalt appeal to thy parental units for much money. If thine request is denied, then thou shalt be content to attend the local community college. And though their athletic program stinketh and you shalt have no team for which to cheer, go thou anyway. And this shall be a sign. You shall find a bundle of checks wrapped in a scholarship envelope. "Go," the Lord says. "And fear not."

Knowing that the Bible wasn't written to specifically address every single situation in life doesn't mean, however, that it has nothing to say on the matter. There are general principles found in Scripture that can guide us. For example, the Bible encourages us to "delight yourself in the LORD, and he will give you the desires of your heart" (Ps. 37:4). In other words, generally speaking, love God with all your heart, and then do what you want, having faith and confidence that (again, *generally* speaking) God will give you the desires He wants you to have.

What do you do if you don't know what you want? In that case, you may want to check out some broad principles, ones that talk about common sense and good judgment (see Acts 15:28-29), or check with some wise people (see Prov. 11:14). In the end, God most likely won't give you specific guidance that you'll find in a fortune cookie or see spelled out in your alphabet cereal. You'll have to make an informed decision by faith, choosing to believe God won't let you deviate from what is best for you.

The alternative (in a situation where the Bible appears to be silent in the specifics) is to follow what you believe the Holy Spirit is saying to your spirit. Now we're back to that mystical element of our faith, one we're generally uncomfortable with. Granted, it's not as concrete as a Bible verse; but in the absence of precise biblical direction, it's just as real and valid. This too requires faith on your part.

You just can't avoid the faith factor in any of these mysteries.

Which reminds me of one more brief mystery about the Bible and you: Sometimes when reading Scripture, you come across a verse or story you've read dozens of times before, but this time it's different somehow. This time it's saying something else to you, something fresh, something for today. This doesn't invalidate your previous encounters with the passage or make the Bible into a glorified horoscope, and this doesn't mean that the original, or primary, meaning of the passage should be dismissed. It's simply evidence that the Word really is "living and active" (Heb. 4:12). It's like the Bible is a multidimensional diamond, and each time you look at it, the Holy Spirit turns each verse slightly, shining a fresh light on it (see John 14:26). A special word for *today*—for *you*.

That's when God wants you to take that word and chew on it, assimilating it into your life experience.

The Download

We've talked about why the Bible is such a mystery to most people. We've also discussed the mystery of how God wrote it and how we interact with it. About these things, there will always be an element of the unknown. No one has yet to completely master the Bible. Not a soul. There are things about this unique Book that will always puzzle you. You might always be tempted to search for that elusive foolproof method for cracking the Bible code, some secret way of unlocking the full meaning of every verse, but if you could do that, you'd rob eternity itself of mystery.

But in light of all this, there are many things concerning the Bible about which there is no mystery and about which we *can* be certain. There are some things that are not a mystery.

God is the same today as He was when He interacted with those throughout biblical history (see 1 Sam. 15:29; Mal. 3:6). Human nature is also the same—we still experience defeats, exploits, failures and accomplishments. And our ability to relate to humanity is the same as well. The disappointment and disillusionment we feel when a celebrated Christian is exposed in a public scandal also envelops us when we read of David's affair with Bathsheba (see 2 Sam. 11). In the same way, we cheer as much over Peter's restoration (see John 21:15-23) or Lazarus's return from the dead (see John 11:1-43) as we do when our favorite movie action-hero escapes from captivity to save the country from a terrorist attack. God wrote the Bible so that we could *connect* with the people found within its pages. And so that we could connect with Him.

Another thing that hasn't changed is that truth is still truth; with the Bible, though, you get an added bonus. Not only can you see the original truth in Scripture, but also (and much like a software update) your experience of that truth is updated as you download it into your life. There's nothing magical about the English words on the pages of your Bible. It's not a book that casts spells or grants them. Rather, those letters, words, paragraphs and books express God's eternal truth—truth that cannot be contained in a leather-bound document. It's bigger than that—and much greater. That's why the truth translates beyond the pages of your Bible and transfers to your heart and life. Only something alive can do that (see Heb. 4:12).

Remember, too, that the Holy Spirit's role is to make the Bible much more than simply a book or collection of great moral lessons. That's precisely why it is so difficult for someone who doesn't have a relationship with Christ to accept the Bible as the written expression of God to humankind (see 1 Cor. 2:14). Without God's Spirit in the picture, there's none of that relational and mystical connection to the Bible.

* * *

There's no need to be intimidated by the Bible—it's *not* like the inside of a computer. And the next time you open up your Bible, see it *not* as a textbook merely to be studied, analyzed, diagrammed, organized and systematized. Don't see the verses as text. Instead, open your eyes wider. See those verses as a passionate God's expression of love to you, a part of a bigger story He has told and is telling. And receive His Word as it really is: creative, compelling, convicting and consuming.

Anything *but* an ancient code.

THE CASE OF THE DISAPPEARING BRIDE

THE MYSTERY OF THE RAPTURE

Listen, I tell you a mystery.

1 Corinthians 15:51

Many years ago, in the months leading up to our wedding day, my wife, Beverly, decided to rummage around in her grandmother's attic one last time. It was a hobby she had enjoyed since childhood. And for good reason. Previous adventures in the old attic had yielded great spoils. Like the diamond watch she once found in a box of trinkets. Or the small stash of European currency she came across.

There were other treasures as well: forgotten family artifacts, old phonograph records, documents, diaries, and dilapidated furniture—everything you might expect after years of storage. For hours, she would sit alone in the old attic—reading, discovering, imagining—a single beam of sunlight streaming through the only window, its rays illuminating the dusty wood floor.

While snooping around that particular day, she spotted something covered in a linen sheet peeking out from a dark corner, something she had never noticed before. She carefully uncovered the object to discover an oil portrait of a very beautiful young woman. The gold-colored frame had a large crack; and the canvas, with an erratic pattern of cracks that resembled a dry lakebed, bore the wear and tear of time. There was also a small gash in the canvas, across a portion of the woman's face, a face that somehow seemed strangely familiar, though Beverly couldn't make a connection.

Hauling the portrait downstairs for a better look, she noticed other details about the woman. She wore a green velvet dress trimmed in lace, and a wine-colored cloak settled softly around her arms. An elegant red-coral necklace highlighted the drop of her neckline. Her hair was pulled back from her fair-skinned face, forming a neat bunch on the back of her neck.

Her lips were highlighted with a rose-colored shade.

But there was one characteristic of this young woman that stood out beyond all the rest: her eyes. She had big blue eyes, deep and radiant. Eyes that followed you regardless of where you stood. Eyes that seemed to look through you, causing the painting to almost come to life. But who was this familiar-looking woman?

Her intrigue now heightened by the hidden identity of the woman in the portrait, Beverly began questioning relatives.

It turns out that the name of the woman in the portrait was Grace Worthington. She had sailed across the ocean from England to New York in the 1830s to meet her fiancé. Just 16 years old when she stepped off a passenger ship in New York Harbor, Grace was met by her fiancé, and the couple then spent a short time seeing the city before making the long journey home. Smitten by the breathtaking sight of his soon-to-be bride, Mr. Worthington insisted that her beauty be captured in portrait form before they left the city. So Grace posed patiently for an artist while her future husband looked on. It would prove to be a portrait as worthy and pleasing as her very name.

As for that curious resemblance? Shortly after being discovered in the attic, Grace's portrait was placed in my future in-law's living room until we moved into our own home. Just prior to our wedding, my wife's brother walked into the room and upon noticing the portrait for the first time, exclaimed without hesitation, "Hey, where did you guys get that painting of Beverly?"

Suddenly, the familiarity of the portrait became clear. Almost magically, everyone could see it, as if a veil had been lifted. A collective chill enveloped us. We all rushed toward the painting for a closer look. There was no denying the details: the big blue eyes, the dark hair, the fair skin, that distinguished English nose, the shape of her lips, the arch of her eyebrow. More than 150 years between them, one young woman extraordinarily mirrored the image of the other. Two brides, separated by a century and a half, peculiarly united just before their wedding days. The past had reached forward to touch the present.

Here Comes the Groom

Jesus was a big fan of weddings and was well aware of their importance to His culture. The ceremony. The customs. The commitment. More than anyone, He understood that the joining of two lives together in marriage can be among the highest points of our earthly existence (see Matt. 19:4-6). He knows this because He made up the idea!

Though formally trained as a carpenter, Jesus was also a master communicator by nature. He knew exactly how to connect with His audience (as well as how to veil the truth from them, as we saw in chapter 4). Part of His genius is found in the culturally relevant images He used. In other words, He was very in touch with the times in which He lived. Almost always dipping into contemporary culture, Jesus painted word portraits, using tons of illustrations, similes and historical references. The result was that the brush-stroked image on His canvas made sense to His hearers. Sadly, we often fail to connect with the Bible because of our unfamiliarity with the customs and traditions of first-century Palestine. Still, that was Jesus' world and, being a good missionary, He knew it well.

One of the customs of Jesus' day involved the events surrounding a traditional Jewish wedding. Jesus' affinity for weddings is evident, not only because He used them as a backdrop for teaching His disciples, but also because He told parables about them (see Matt. 22:1-14; 25:1-13). He even chose to perform His very first recorded miracle at a wedding (see John 2:1-11). Fast-forward to His last night with His closest friends, the eve before His crucifixion. It was a time when the disciples' world was about to deconstruct around them, and Jesus needed a way to help them cope with the fact that He was about to leave them. So He decided to write a covenant song in their hearts, using the Jewish wedding motif as His guiding melody.

Jewish couples in those days were engaged up to 24 months before their actual wedding day (there was no Las Vegas). The man would propose a written covenant (called a *ketubah*) to the bride-to-be and her father, outlining his intentions for marriage. At this time, he also presented the father with a gift to compensate him for the cost of raising her. If this proposal were accepted, the man poured a cup of wine (representing a blood covenant) for the girl and waited to see if she took it. Drinking the cup meant she accepted the proposal, and they were now betrothed. The young woman then spent the next 12 to 24 months making herself ready and remaining pure and beautiful for her husband. As she anticipated the day when her fiancé would return and get her, she wore a veil in public, so others would know she was spoken for (or "bought with a price").[1]

This engagement period was legally binding, though there was no physical intimacy during this time. But in other ways, they were already considered as good as married. They even paid taxes as a couple. This extended betrothal period allowed plenty of time to plan the wedding, but it also ensured the man that his fiancée was not with child. In the event she turned up pregnant during this time, the man could break the engagement through a legal "letter of divorce" (Matt. 5:31, *NLT*). You may recall that Joseph, upon discovering Mary was pregnant with Jesus, decided to divorce her secretly so that she wouldn't be disgraced (see Matt. 1:19). Fortunately for Mary, an angel visited her fiancé and convinced him that the child was "from the Holy Spirit" (Matt. 1:20).

It was also during this long engagement period that the groom returned to his father's house. There he prepared a honeymoon room for his bride; this is where the couple typically stayed for seven days following the wedding. Until the wedding day, the woman clung to the man's promise to come and claim his bride at an appointed time, a time known only by his father. Just before midnight on the night of their wedding, the night chosen by the groom's father, the groomsmen would run ahead to the bride's house, shouting and sounding the shofar (a trumpetlike instrument usually made from a ram's horn).

The groom then whisked his bride back to his father's house where the couple consummated the marriage, after which the groom informed the best man, who would, in turn, announce the good news to the wedding guests. Then everybody basically partied for seven days. Sounds like fun, huh?

Jesus' disciples were all familiar with these wedding customs and protocols, some of the disciples surely having experienced a wedding themselves. So they could relate to what Jesus said to them during their last meal together:

Do not let your hearts be troubled. Trust in God; trust also in Me. In *my Father's house* are many *rooms*; if it were not so, I would have told you. I am going there to *prepare a place for you*. And if I go and prepare a place for you, *I will come back and take you to be with me* that you also may be where I am (John 14:1-3, emphasis added).

As you might guess, for the disciples, the thought of Jesus' leaving them was not only unacceptable but also unimaginable. It was not something they had ever contemplated, much less something they were ready to receive. He was their Rabbi, Master, Savior and Friend. Jesus had not only taught them about life—He *was* their life (see John 6:67-69; 14:6)! They had spent the last three years together with Him—traveling, eating, spreading the good news, casting out demons, healing diseases, bonding—doing life together. These guys had history. They were a team. They were tight.

Now all of a sudden Jesus was telling them that they couldn't go with Him anymore (see John 13:33,36). The look of disbelief on their faces must have told the story of what they were feeling in their hearts: *Wait a minute, Lord. Let me get this straight. You're leaving us? C'mon, You can't be serious. I don't understand. Did we do something wrong? Are You firing us? Have You found new disciples? Tell us You're kidding . . . please!*

All they had experienced with Jesus was unexpectedly coming to an abrupt end. And the news was devastating

But like other times, the truth of what Jesus said didn't really sink in until much later. His words, though simple, were meaty and took time to digest. Consider the following paraphrase:

Guys, gather around for a minute. We need to talk. It hurts Me to tell you this, but I'm going away for a while. A long while. You know that wine we just drank together? That was like the wine a man gives his fiancée when they get engaged. And I am going away to My Father's house just like the groom does. I have to go so that I can prepare a special place for you. But I will come back to get you. I promise. And then we'll be together again, this time forever. As proof, I'm sending the Holy Spirit to live in you until I come again.

As expected, this Holy Spirit concept was repeated to the disciples before they began to get it (see John 15:26-27; 16:7-15; 20:22-23). Following His resurrection, Jesus did physically leave the Earth, just like He said He would (see Acts 1:9-11). We can all agree on that. He's currently now in heaven (see Heb. 1:3; 8:1; 12:2). But before He left, He used this wedding word picture to assure His followers that they'd see Him again one day.

But here's the question that hovered in the minds of the original Twelve and that has hovered in the minds of every disciple since then: *When is Jesus coming back?* (See John 16:17-18.) There's a corollary question: *How will it happen?* That's the double-edged mystery here.

Drawing from Jesus' own words, along with other passages in Scripture, a belief was born among some Christians concerning what may be the next red-letter date on God's personal calendar. Most call it the Rapture, when Jesus suddenly returns to snatch up His Bride (the Church) and take Her to heaven to live with Him. For the last 2,000 years, He's been there preparing a special place for us. For those who believe in the Rapture, this return isn't believed to be the actual Second Coming of Jesus to Earth described in other parts of Scripture, but instead is thought to be a midair reunion of Bride and Groom (see Rev. 19:7-9), a long-awaited wedding day.

Here's how Paul describes it:

> Brothers, we do not want you to be ignorant about those who fall asleep, or to grieve like the rest of men, who have no hope. We believe that Jesus died and rose again and so we believe that God will bring with Jesus those who have fallen asleep in him. According to the Lord's own word, we tell you that we who are still alive, who are left till the coming of the Lord, will certainly not precede those who have fallen asleep. For the Lord himself will come down from heaven, with a *loud command,* with the *voice of the archangel* and with the *trumpet call of God,* and the dead in Christ will rise first. After that, we who are still alive and are left will be *caught up* together with them in the clouds to meet the Lord in the air. And so *we will be with the Lord* forever. Therefore encourage each other with these words (1 Thess. 4:13-18, emphasis added).

Apparently, to the Christians living in first-century Thessalonica, there was confusion about what had happened to fellow believers who had died. Where had they gone? Would they ever be seen again? So Paul tells them that our grieving over the dead in Christ is made worse if there's no hope of ever seeing them again. But that's not the case! Those who have died are currently with the Lord (see 2 Cor. 5:8), and when Jesus comes from heaven (that is, the Father's house), He will bring those departed spirits with Him.

This appearance will be accompanied by "a *loud command*, with the *voice* of the archangel and with the *trumpet* call of God." Sounds eerily parallel to the wedding announcement of the bridegroom, doesn't it? Then we (the Bride of Christ) "will be *caught up* together" with the decomposed bodies of those who have waited for redemption. Those bodies will be restored to a resurrected state and will be reunited with their spirits from heaven. And the purpose? To "*be with the Lord* [our Bridegroom] *forever*" in the Father's house, of course.

The mystery of this event is that although some will sleep (die), others will be alive to witness this event. Still, *all* "will be changed" (1 Cor. 15:52). Adding to the mystery is that this entire sequence—the command, the voice, the trumpet, the Lord appearing, Christians lifted up, corpses bursting out of their graves, a mass reunion in the sky, everyone being transformed into bodies that defy death and decay—all will happen "in a flash, in the twinkling of an eye" (1 Cor. 15:52). As quick as thought. As fast as the speed of light. Faster.

It's estimated that the average blink of an eye lasts between three and four hundred milliseconds (or about three-tenths of a second). But a twinkle is believed to last only about one hundred milliseconds (or one-tenth of a second). That's pretty quick. Paul was trying to communicate that this event will happen so fast, it will be virtually instantaneous. In other words, it will occur in an infinitesimal space of time, so small a period of time that it cannot be measured. Faster than the time it takes to think it, it's already in the past tense.

That's more than mysterious. That's freaky.

But wait a millisecond here, you might be thinking. *I don't see the word "rapture" in those verses.*

Right, you don't. And you won't find it anywhere else in the Bible, either. But then, you also won't find the words "trinity," "theology," "divinity," "atheist" or even "Bible"! Actually, no modern English words are in the original Scriptures. Through translation, we've substituted English equivalents for words and phrases found in the original written languages of the Bible. In this case, the phrase "caught up" is translated from *harpazo,* a Greek word that means "snatch away." We get our word "rapture" from the Latin translation of that Greek word. Paul used the same word in 2 Corinthians 12:2 when describing his experience of being "caught up to the third heaven." Exact same word—different event. (Besides, "The Rapture" sounds a lot better than "The Snatching," which sounds like a horror movie.)

The Next Big Thing

I keep a calendar on my laptop. Lots of people do. It comes in handy for folks like me who tend to forget things. Maybe you keep a calendar, too. If so, you probably fill it with stuff like appointments, dates, meetings, trips, birthdays, speaking engagements and other things you don't want to forget to do.

I suspect God must keep a calendar, too. I think He writes on it special dates and events, appointments He has with humanity, along with a list of tasks to be completed in space and time.

Open up His past date books and you'll find some of those red-letter days:

- Monday, January 1, 10,000 B.C., 6:00 A.M.—Create the heavens and Earth. Tell Lucifer, "You're fired!"

- Tuesday, January 16, 4:00 P.M.—Meet with Adam/Eve re: fruit episode

You get the idea. I imagine there have been other significant dates on His calendar as well: Israel's deliverance from Egypt, the birth of Christ, Jesus' crucifixion and resurrection, the coming of the Holy Spirit, and if you're Protestant, that infamous day in 1517 when Martin Luther nailed his 95 theses to the church door of Wittenberg, Germany.

But the question now is, What's next on God's calendar? What's the next biggie on His to-do list? Is it the Rapture? Is there such a thing, or have we conjured it up out of our sanctified imaginations and hope of escaping what we believe is a coming world chaos? Is it merely some romantic ideal we've created because we don't want to be here when the world goes nuts? Will God rescue His Bride before the so-called Great Tribulation? After all, He rescued Noah and his family prior to the Flood, He got Lot out of Sodom and Gomorrah, and He saved Rahab from the destruction of Jericho. And the Bible says He's going to deliver us from "the coming wrath" (1 Thess. 1:10; see also Rom. 5:9; 1 Thess: 5:9).

On the other hand, you could argue that although some in the Bible were spared from suffering and martyrdom (like

Daniel, Shadrach and friends), most actually ended up going through the fire (like Jeremiah, Isaiah, Job, Stephen and Paul). So maybe our confidence in the Rapture's reality isn't so much an issue of God's past pattern of behavior. Instead, maybe our question should be, *What does God say He's going to do?* In other words, our confidence should lie in those Bible passages that point toward the Rapture, not in the assumption that just because He did it for Daniel and Lot, He'll do it for us.

Keep in mind: There are great scholars, sincere theologians and godly people who respectfully disagree on the Rapture question. Your view may differ from mine, depending on your denomination or church affiliation. And that's okay. Bigger than who's right and who's wrong is letting God be God in the matter. As for me, I believe it will happen. I just think there's a lot more mystery to it than most of us are willing to admit.

Regardless of your view, it's still a fascinating concept, this snatching up of Christians off the planet. Just the thought of millions of people literally disappearing into thin air and the chaos that would follow sparks the curiosity of most people, so much so that over 60 million copies of the *Left Behind* series have been sold. Is it possible this series was woven into God's plan to help prepare His Bride for the return of Her Bridegroom? Could there be a future reality far more real than what's portrayed in speculative novels found in the Christian section at Barnes and Noble? And what's the deal with the perceived proximity of the Rapture? Could it really happen soon? Tomorrow?

The first-century disciples thought they'd see their Lord return before they saw death. And for the past few hundred years, every generation has thought *they* were the generation that would meet Him in the air. What ruins it for me is that every few years some crackpot preacher claims he's hacked into God's hard drive and stolen the launch codes for Jesus' return to planet Earth. Some madmen have even held watch parties, climbing to mountaintops, hoping they'd be the first to be taken. But Jesus has been a no-show for every one of these parties. The Rapture's timing is (and remains) privileged information. Top Secret. Classified. For God's eyes only.

More fuel for the mystery.

The Inspiration of Hope

In the months leading up to my wedding, I joined a gym. I signed a contract promising to give them something like $50 a month in exchange for the privilege of sweating inside their building. I was determined to have a body deserving of the beautiful bride whom I was about to marry. I also didn't want her to think she had married a loser. So I hit the weight room and began working out regularly: curls, squats, bench presses, military presses. I did whatever it took, adopting the then-popular "No Pain, No Gain" philosophy. Several times a week, I tortured my body while my fellow weight lifters screamed "encouragement" at me: "C'mon, Kinley! You can do it! Don't be a girly-man! Pump it! Just one more! You can do it!"

The result was that by the day of my wedding, I was, shall we say, buff. I was lifting and benching more weight than at any time in my life, before or since. I had a well-defined physique.

But that, as they say, was then. This is now. Don't misunderstand. I'm no Jabba the Hutt today. I'm just not the same physical specimen I was at 22. Hey, but who is? I was just doing my part to get ready for the big day.

If you're married, you understand what a monumental day this is. If you're not, just take my word for it. Typically set at least six months out, this red-letter date becomes etched in stone. Changing it would probably require an act of Congress and certainly a box of tissues. Groomsmen and bridesmaids make travel plans. Hundreds of invitations are designed, printed and sent. A location is reserved. The minister is secured. Cakes are ordered. Vows are written. Flowers are chosen. Rings are picked out and purchased. A photographer is hired, and maybe a videographer. A caterer and menu are selected. Then there's the reception band to be booked. Groomsmen and bridesmaids gifts are bought. Other wedding party participants, along with extended family members, receive special invitations to the reception. Honeymoon hotel reservations are made. Plane tickets are bought. Travel clothes are packed. Appointments are made for the bride to get special hair and beauty treatments on the day of her wedding. There are also parties and showers to attend and a host of other things girls do, but I can't say because I'm male, and they don't tell us these things.

If you're a guy, preparing for your wedding is a universe apart from what the girl has to do. If you're a guy, you shower, shave and show up.

For months, it feels like you're an insignificant satellite stuck in orbit around Planet Marriage. It's a day most girls dream of all their lives, and a day bride and groom will remember forever. Everything else on your calendar takes a back seat to this event.

Matrimony is a big deal and always has been. It's a day filled with great expectancy—and rightly so. It symbolizes a transformation from incompleteness to wholeness. And a day of freedom, too: free to now become all you were meant to be and free to engage in total intimacy with your soul mate.

In the same way, Jesus' return for His Bride also triggers a transformation, this one signaling the end of death's power over us. At the Rapture, death will be declawed, its stinger forever removed (see 1 Cor. 15:55). It no longer will take anything or anyone from us. And no longer will our selfish nature plague us with its sin-bent ways. Gone forever will be our daily struggle with hypocrisy. No more temptation. No more guilt. No more shame.

But greater than all of these will be the one thing for which we've waited all these years, the one thing more anticipated than anything else, greater than our freedom from the bonds of earthly living and more exciting than stepping onto heaven's shore: At the very instant we are caught up in the sky, we will actually meet the Lord face to face for the first time (see 1 Thess. 4:16). I am powerless to create a mental image of what that will look like or imagine what my soul will feel in that moment. But as my friend Bart Millard so appropriately wrote:

Surrounded by Your Glory, what will my heart feel?
Will I dance for You, Jesus? Or in awe of You be still?
Will I stand in Your presence, or to my knees will I fall?
Will I sing "Hallelujah!"? Will I be able to speak at all?
I can only imagine! I can only imagine![2]

In that instant, we will "see him just as he is" (1 John 3:2). No family Bible artwork and no Hollywood portrayals this time. Just Jesus, the Lover of our souls. His heart touching ours.

And nothing else will matter in that moment. The pressures and stresses of life—school, job, bills, debt, traffic, mean people—all will be gone forever from our experience.

* * *

You can begin to understand why Paul was compelled to conclude his words on this subject by writing:

> Therefore encourage each another with these words (1 Thess. 4:18).

> Therefore, my dear brothers, stand firm. Let nothing move you. Always give yourselves fully to the work of the Lord, because you know that your labor in the Lord is not in vain (1 Cor. 15:58).

The mystery of the Rapture compels us to embrace the hope it inspires among those who believe, hope that the Bridegroom is coming. So make yourself ready.

But it also infuses us with confidence, a settled belief that no good deed, however small or insignificant, will go unrewarded. So don't give up.

This mystery also catapults us into the consummation of a divine romance. It's the culmination of life's greatest love story, a crescendo of emotion that no earthly relationship has ever known. And never has a Groom been so excited to see His Bride.

Only this time she's more than a bride called Grace.

She's the Bride called by Grace.

Notes

1. "Jewish Life Cycles: Engagement, Marriage and Divorce" at becomingjewish.com. http://www.becomingjewish.org/jlife.html (accessed July 2007).

2. Bart Millard, "I Can Only Imagine" ©2001 Simpleville Music. All rights reserved. Used by permission.

CHAPTER 9

BEWARE THE SEVEN SEALS

THE MYSTERY OF THE END TIMES

The mystery of God will be accomplished.

Revelation 10:7

Standing in my kitchen one summer afternoon years ago, I was unprepared for the strange noise coming from our living room. Of course, strange sounds are not uncommon around here. I live in a home filled with unexplained noises. Eventually, most of these odd audibles have a perfectly rational explanation. For example, once I heard a loud hissing sound coming from my study. Relatively confident I didn't own an Egyptian cobra, I cautiously peered around the doorway for a closer look. Upon peeking in, the source of the noise became apparent: Water was gushing from the ceiling above and crashing onto the hardwood floor, producing a sound similar to what you hear while camping beside a mountain stream.

But it wasn't a hissing sound I heard that summer afternoon. Nor was it anywhere close to the usual creaks and groans associated with an old house like ours. Instead, this particular sound was immediately recognizable. It was the chiming of a clock. Which is not that weird, until you understand that we don't own a chiming clock—not one that works anyway. Or at least as far as we knew.

Over time, our home has become the gathering place for old family items, largely due to the fact that my wife can't say no to things that no one else seems to want. It's almost like living in a museum—or more like a graveyard of sorts, the final resting place for dead and discarded relics. As a result, our home carries a certain nineteenth-century charm about it.

Years earlier, we had been given an old clock by a relative who had received it from a great-grandmother. It's a heavy, black mantle clock framed in ebony columns and crowned with a Romanesque roof. When it was given to us, we were told,

"This old thing has never worked. You can have it." Over the months following the chaos of moving in and unpacking, we had lost the key needed to wind it, so it sat silently on a table in our living room, gathering dust. About as functional as a tombstone or a large paperweight, the clock was set by my wife to 11:55, a mute reminder of Jesus words, "As long as it is day, we must do the work of him who sent me. Night is coming, when no one can work" (John 9:4).

But time, dust and the fact that it hadn't been wound in decades didn't stop the old clock from unexpectedly chiming that day. Loudly. Tiptoeing my way through the dining room and into the living room, I stood in silent fear while the clock kept chiming: once, twice, three times, four times, all the way to twelve chimes and then thirteen-o-clock! My eyes widened. I didn't know it could be that late! For a clock thought to be dead, hearing those chimes for the first time captured my attention and also convinced me that you never know when something strange might happen in our house.

It hasn't made a sound since.

Does Anybody Really Know What Time It Is?

When it comes to the topic of the end times, I often think about our old clock and wonder how close to the "midnight hour" we really are. It makes me think about the future—not so much my own destiny, but the future of humankind.

Maybe you're like me and you've read about all these wild prophetic events in the Bible. It's possible you read a Josh McDowell book once and were amazed by the prophecies about the Messiah. And so, armed with your newly discovered truth bullets, you began firing them at unbelieving skeptics in hopes of convincing them to follow Jesus. I must confess, I've never beaten one single person into salvation by lashing them with the prophecy cat-o'-nine-tails. I'm not a big fan of arguing anyone into the Kingdom, actually. This doesn't mean that those fulfilled prophecies are unimportant, only that they make a whole lot more sense to a first-century Jewish audience looking for a Messiah. Their passion in rejecting or accepting those predictive words about Jesus had a lot to do with the fact that it affected them and their lives in their here and now. The closer the perceived proximity of those events to people's lives, the more interest there is likely to be in them. The more contemporary, the more convincing.

That's why I suspect that prophecies regarding the end times arouse serious interest in our current culture. Put simply: People think it might have something to do with them!

Of course, these days you never know what version of the end times you're bound to hear. Similar to the Rapture, views vary regarding the events leading up to the actual Second Coming of Jesus, with everyone bent on franchising their own version of the future. The espousers of each interpretation are convinced that theirs is the right one, each as confident as the next.

Regardless of your position, most everyone agrees that unraveling the mystery to the end-times enigma largely lies in understanding the last book in the Bible. This book (called Revelation) is the written record of a high-resolution vision God gave to the apostle John. This is the same guy who penned the Gospel that bears his name, along with three other short letters included in the New Testament. An old man at the time he wrote Revelation, John was likely in his 90s. (He had no word in his vocabulary for *retirement*.) Still spreading the good news about Jesus well into his golden years, John was arrested and exiled to the desert penal colony of Patmos, an island off the coast of Greece in the Aegean Sea. It's rumored that Emperor Domitian was perturbed because John didn't die when he had him boiled in oil. Legend has it that John continued to preach from the boiling pot! Imagine what this man must have gone through: no medication to relieve his suffering, no skin grafts— just raw, hard-core pain. And what must he have looked like, with most of his body covered in scar tissue? In spite of persecution and torture, he continued loving and living out his faith, so the emperor sentenced him to live out the rest of his days on Patmos, cut off from the world.

But as great as his power was, Domitian couldn't disconnect John's heart from his Savior.

While alone in a cave, John was given by God a vision that would eventually find its way into the Bible. In John's native language, the word we translate as "revelation" means "an unveiling" or "to uncover what has been hidden." In a twist of irony, of all the books in the Bible, this one has remained more veiled, hidden and misunderstood than all the rest combined.

Centuries before John, the prophet Daniel (of the lion's den fame) was instructed to seal up his own prophecies concerning the end times (see Dan. 12:4). In other words, a time would come when the seals of the scrolls would be broken, the scrolls would be unrolled for us to see, and understanding about them would be revealed. Like John's vision, Daniel's prophecy also involved God's wrath (see Dan. 8:19,26).

Is it possible that God has sealed from our understanding the prophecies contained in the books of Daniel and Revelation until the time just prior to their fulfillment? Would that explain the explosive interest and exploration of Revelation in the last several decades? Does this mean we're living in the age of their fulfillment? Are we about to see how the pieces of the puzzle come together, a puzzle God has been assembling behind the scenes for centuries?

Looks Like Rain

As we survey history, we discover we're not the only generation that has imagined themselves experiencing the cataclysmic events spoken of in Revelation. The cruelty and persecution from Roman emperors and the destruction of Jerusalem in the first century certainly bear some resemblance to the events recorded in John's book—in fact, there are some Christians who read the book of Revelation with those tyrants and events in mind. Of course, evil people and rulers have always existed, causing some to speculate if a particular individual was "the man of lawlessness" spoken of in Scripture (2 Thess. 2:3). The Hitlers and Husseins and even certain "holy men" in history have all tried their hand at world domination. But like early contestants on *American Idol*, we've yet to see who'll make it to the final cut.

Conjectures and speculations about the identity of this man only muddy the waters. Paul warned us not to be "unsettled" by the false prophecies of those who would try to alarm us. Prophetic utterances should be viewed with a skeptical eye, and we should be especially wary of preachers in purple suits on TV who profess to have the real scoop on the future; even if someone claims to be speaking with God's authority, don't listen (see 2 Thess. 2:1-3). Human nature often seeks to capitalize on the fears of the weak and uninformed, captivating their attention and amazing them with end-times charts and timelines. But don't be fooled. No matter how persuasive the PowerPoint presentation or how graphic the video, we must be careful and wise.

Still, for me all these counterfeits suggest there is an authentic reality in the future and that humanity is on a collision course with destiny. I am utterly convinced that the end-times story is real, and that it is a story filled with terrible judgment. It contains R-rated subject matter and unpleasant truth that reveals what many feel to be the dark side of God: His wrath. Like many other of His character traits, God's furious anger remains as mysterious and murky as a nineteenth-century London fog. And just as hard to breathe.

Logically, it's difficult to imagine how God can allow evil to flourish. Emotionally, it's hard to imagine a loving God being so vengeful and judging. But love without righteousness is nothing more than sentimental syrup, and a love that never disciplines is merely masked cowardice. Somehow, God is equally loving and wrathful. You and I have to live with that mystery. And so, having given His creation sufficient time and opportunity to repent, I believe God will play hardball in the end times.

It reminds me of the only other time God went postal on His creation. You remember the story of Noah and the Flood, don't you? It's a tale typically reserved for little kids. Churches even construct their children's ministries around its theme: wall murals, stuffed animals, toy boats—you know the drill. I can hear the children's director now, greeting the toddlers on their first day of Sunday School:

> Good morning, children! Welcome to Kid's World. Oh, look over there! What do I see on the wall? Why, it's a boat. A great big boat. And who built that big boat? Anybody know? Right, Noah did! It took Mr. Noah a very long time to build this boat, but he did it because he obeyed God. Do you want to obey God? Sure you do! And look at all the pretty animals coming up the boat ramp, two by two. What animals do you see? I see giraffes and elephants and even some scary tigers. But these tigers are smiling, just like all the other animals. They want to obey God, too! They're very glad to come and ride on Noah's ark.

Are you seasick yet?

I think the story of Noah is anything *but* a children's story. I'm not even sure most adults can handle it! That's because there's a lot more to the story than cute animals and a boat ride. To begin with, things were so bad on the earth in Noah's day that God couldn't even find 10 good people who deserved to live!

> God saw that human evil was out of control. People thought evil, imagined evil—evil, evil, evil from morning to night. God was sorry that he had made the human

race in the first place; it broke his heart. God said, "I'll get rid of my ruined creation, make a clean sweep: people, animals, snakes and bugs, birds—the works. I'm sorry I made them" (Gen. 6:5-7,11-12, *THE MESSAGE*)

Holy cow! Can you picture that? Can you comprehend the entire human race imagining only evil 24 hours a day? Not one person thinking a single good or decent thought? Nobody? Can you also begin to imagine God saying to His creation, "I'm sorry you were ever born"? I mean, this must have been a tough call for the Lord, wiping out the only creation made in His image.

But though He grieved over humankind's condition, God did not retreat into a corner to sulk or throw a pity party for Himself. God's sadness was a mixed drink of sorrow, wrath and grace. He decided to destroy everyone and everything—all people, regardless of social status, age or gender . . . and even the animals!

Instead of simply annihilating them with a lightning bolt or a huge meteor, blasting them into a vapor, God planned a slower and more surprising demise. He promised to send a flood, something Earth's residents had no doubt never seen before. In fact, they had never even seen rain up to that point (see Gen. 2:4-5). But rain it did, producing a great deluge that drowned an entire planet.

The first time I heard this story, I was eight years old. Our family was camping by a big lake not far from our home. It was late at night, and a huge rainstorm was pouring down outside. Lightning flashed all around us, thunder seemed to shake the ground, and the wind whipped wildly around our thick canvas tent. My teenage cousin had the bright idea that this would be the perfect time to tell me the story of the Great Flood. In my faded memory, I somehow remember her beginning with, "It was a night just like tonight . . ."

As she spoke, I could see in my mind's eye the people of Noah's day frantically climbing trees to escape the rising waters. I imagined them panicking, clawing their way up hills and mountains, racing into caves, looking for safety. I saw the terror on their faces as they realized there was no higher ground left. I pictured a mob gripped with mass hysteria, killing one other in an attempt to make it to dry ground, cursing God and one another with their last breath.

And as the rain continued to pelt our tent, I swallowed hard, convinced *we* were next on God's list to exterminate.

Then cousin Carol told me about God's promise and the whole rainbow thing and I was alright after that.

Picture this if you can: When the Flood came, it must have been like a world tsunami, and the carnage would have been more horrifying than any human disaster you or I have ever witnessed or seen on the big screen (see Gen. 7:11-12). The celestial floodgates above were opened and massive sheets of water fell on the earth. Combined with this were gargantuan underground springs bursting up like geysers. This went on nonstop for 40 days and 40 nights. Only Noah and his family were saved (and even they weren't all that righteous) (see Gen. 9:18-25).

Unless we know the full story of the Flood, we might be tempted to think this event was some sort of divine temper tantrum thrown by God. But a closer look reveals another story. For starters, it took Noah 120 years to build his aircraft-carrier-sized ark, and you can bet that during that time, people took notice of what Noah was doing. His big boat was without a doubt the talk of the region and possibly the entire world as far as we know. And that's part of the point: Noah made sure people were warned of God's coming judgment (see 2 Pet. 2:5, *NLT*), and for 120 years, people had the opportunity to turn to God. Grace was still offered, and escaping judgment was still just a prayer away.

There is one more piece of evidence of mercy in the midst of God's impending condemnation, one that is rarely mentioned when the story of Noah is told, one more indication that God gave humans more than enough time to repent. As the master storyteller and ultimate suspense novelist, the Most High wrote a subtle twist into the script. It has to do with someone you've probably heard of, a background character whose role becomes much clearer to us in hindsight. His name was Methuselah, and you may remember him as the oldest living person in the Bible (or anywhere else!). This guy hung around Earth for 969 years! Of course, everyone was living longer before the Flood. But at 969 years, Methuselah wins the prize.

For the longest time, Methuselah has been nothing more than a name used in geriatric jokes (as in, "He's as old as Methuselah!"). But he was also Noah's grandfather and the son of a man named Enoch. Enoch was a prophet and a man so godly that he skipped death and went straight to heaven (see Gen. 5:24). You might even say he was raptured! (Enoch is a mystery for another time.)

Even though Methuselah lived longer than anyone else, the length of his life isn't really what's so amazing. Rather, it's the *meaning* of his name. "Methuselah" literally means "when he is gone, it shall be sent" or "his death shall bring it." Bring what? What is sent when Methuselah is gone? When we do the simple math from the birth records in Genesis, we discover that the Flood came when Noah was 600 years old. Big deal, right?

Actually, it *is* a big deal when you realize that it's also the exact year Methuselah died. In other words, God sent a warning to Earth, not in the form of a highway billboard or church sign, but in a man's name. As long as Methuselah was alive, there would be no Flood. As long as he was breathing, judgment would be delayed. Every time his mom called him for dinner, every time a friend said hello to him, the prophecy Enoch embedded in his son's name was announced to his culture. Each time "Methuselah" was heard, God broadcast a message of grace to the human race. And the longer this man lived, the more famous his name must have become.

Of course, it's possible that every single person didn't understand what "Methuselah" meant. On the other hand, maybe they did. Maybe that's why he lived so long, protected by people who were very motivated to keep him alive and judgment far away.

Then again, maybe they knew and just didn't care.

Whatever the case, in the same year Methuselah died, the Flood came—just like God's prophet said it would. Coincidence? Of course I can't prove it, but it's my suspicion that the second Noah lowered his granddad's almost-millennium-aged body into the ground, a lone drop of rain made its long journey downward from the dark gray sky and splashed heavily onto the boat builder's nose. And that may have been his cue to quickly load the family into the ark and prepare for the Flood.

Once inside, God Himself shut the door to the ark (see Gen. 7:16). It was at this moment that the truth must have finally dawned on those outside the ark. "It's real! Crazy old Noah was right after all! Everything he said is coming true!" And they sprinted or dog-paddled their way to the massive wooden ship and began banging on the door, pleading to be let onboard. But the door had been sealed so tight that no water could get in. No people either. Noah could no more open that huge door than he could have closed it. It was locked tight, and God alone knew the combination. And every living thing that breathed on the earth was killed.

Sound like a children's story to you?

Déjà Vu?

Jesus drew a parallel between the days of Noah and the days leading up to the end times and His return (see Matt. 24:37-39). He said that people will simply be going about their business, just living their lives for themselves, without even a thought about God or eternity. And then suddenly, like the Flood, judgment will come. And nothing will be able to stop it.

I believe God is bringing history to a climactic end. When, I don't know. But doomsday scenarios, global disasters, tsunamis, meteors, earthquakes, diseases, global terrorism and threats of nuclear war are more possible now than at any time in history. Is that just a coincidence? Or is it something more, like maybe clouds gathering? The worst that humankind has imagined in disaster movies, many Christians believe Scripture predicts that worse will be experienced in real time, an apocalyptic screenplay with God Himself directing the epic.

According to a literal reading of Revelation, God's judgments will come via the imagery immediately familiar to John's first-century audience: Seals to sacred documents are broken and judgments are read. Trumpets sound, announcing the arrival of more catastrophes. Incense bowls filled with God's furious anger are poured out on Earth and humanity. Wars, economic collapse, plagues, famine, solar eclipses, meteors, earthquakes, fiery hail, oceans and drinking water contaminated, demonic creatures set free from prison to torment mankind, death angels released, persecution and execution of Christians reinstated. The anti-Christ is revealed, establishing himself as world leader, economic savior and global peacemaker. Partnering with him is a counterfeit miracle worker ("the false prophet" [Rev. 19:20]), deceiving the world with his paranormal illusions (see 2 Thess. 2:9). Together they pursue their selfish quest for world domination and destruction of everything that smells of the true God. All the while, God's judgments continue. And billions are destroyed. It's all there in the Book, and one day it will be playing in a neighborhood near you.

This scenario, if read as even remotely literal, does not make our world's prospects for a bright future very likely. In His infinite complexity, Yahweh is as much wrath and retribution as He is mercy and love. You can theologize all you like about that fact, but you will never wrap your arms around it.

But this same God is also patient—very patient. You might even say He has shown great tolerance for humanity by withholding judgment for over 2,000 years. Even His prolonged patience, however, has a limit to how long it will delay humankind's deserved end. There are boundaries He has set. If the events recorded in John's vision are true, our world had better brace itself for a cataclysmic showdown. God's anger, dammed up like a mighty river for centuries, will finally be unleashed into the Valley of Mankind, cutting a bloody swath of death, destruction and delirium.

Part of this judgment is that God releases humankind to *themselves* without restraint. Finally humanity will receive the gift it has longed for throughout history: a world without God. Humankind will devolve even further, making a wild weekend in Las Vegas look like a church service in comparison. *Every* city will become Sin City. This is what the Bible calls "the mystery of lawlessness" (2 Thess. 2:7, *NASB*). As in Noah's day, all that will be left behind are those "who have not believed the truth but have delighted in wickedness" (see 2 Thess. 2:12). The only signs of moral sanity will be the faint echoes of conscience carried over from a time when God's Spirit dwelled on the earth. But that time will be no more.

This mystery is a foreboding one. And although it is not fully understood, two things are clearly revealed: humankind's inherent capacity for evil and God's capacity for retribution.

There are few, if any, warm fuzzies in this end-times scenario. There is, however, a reverential fear that wraps me like a wool blanket as I read Revelation—an appropriate trembling as I contemplate a God who would, could and will do these things to His creation:

Fear God and give him glory, because the hour of his judgment has come. Worship him who made the heavens, the earth, the sea and the springs of water (Rev. 14:7).

191

Missing the Point

But are there any signs that we are living at the threshold of these end times? And if so, are those signs found only by unraveling the minutia of John's Revelation message? Or is it possible that the mystery of Earth's last days isn't understood by identifying the tenth horn or the fourth head of the beast coming up out of the sea (see Rev. 12:3; 13:1; 17:3)? Instead, what if the mystery is better understood by looking at the big picture? Maybe rather than microscopically picking apart the details of Daniel and Revelation, taking a panoramic view of God's drama with humankind would make the last days clearer. The devil may indeed be in the details, but God might be found in the panoramic view.

A while back I was visiting my good friend Peter Wade, a pastor in the historic town of Coleford, not far from London. While walking through the vegetable section at a market near his home, I was joking with him about the Euro currency and the likelihood of the anti-Christ coming to power through the European Union.

"You Americans," he laughed, while picking up some squash, "you're always so obsessed with identifying the seventh horn on the fourth beast that you've missed the whole point. Christ is returning, and we should prepare ourselves for His arrival. On this side of the Pond, I feel I've won a victory if I can convince my people He's actually coming back at all!"

I agree with Peter. We can spend so much energy in research that we become academic Christians, missing the point. Lost in the pursuit of prophecy and its interpretation, we forget to keep moving forward, loving God and loving our neighbor in the name of Jesus.

Remember, the prophecies concerning Jesus' first coming were given so that His people could prepare for Him and recognize Him when He showed up. Yet no one really understood the details of His first coming *until* He arrived. God waited until Jesus' actual coming before allowing people to get it. And even then, the people didn't understand all the prophesies until later on.

I mean, suppose we were able to know the identity of leaders and nations mentioned in Revelation. What difference would it really make, other than making us feel smarter? Is enjoying the satisfaction of "I told you so" what we're really seeking? Does the pursuit of the interpretation of prophecy cater more to our hearts or to our egos? And how could we ever be 100-percent certain we're right unless we're left behind to confirm these prophecies?

Maybe God will unveil all these prophecies suddenly at the actual time of their fulfillment. Maybe in the end times, He'll turn the light switch on, leapfrogging us toward solving the apocalyptic puzzle. Who knows?

* * *

Of course, God has not left us completely in the dark concerning the last days. Despite the weird imagery of an old man's vision, Revelation indicates that a desperate hour in humanity is approaching. How soon, no one is sure. I think it might be sooner than any of us realize, but I'm convinced that our task is not to identify future characters and solve all the riddles of Revelation, but to identify with the Christ who is coming.

If we continue walking through the haze of prophecy, we eventually arrive at the end of the Book. There, at the finish line of our earthly race, we find the one thing that matters more than anything else: the One who controls it all. And for those who seek that Christ, our adventure ultimately concludes with great hope and an unimaginable, bright future. It's He who has wound Earth's old clock. And it's He who will cause it to strike at the appointed time.

Are you listening?

Are you ready?

CHAPTER 10

THE CURSE OF THE FORGOTTEN PEOPLE

THE MYSTERY OF ISRAEL

*I do not want you to be ignorant
of this mystery.*

Romans 11:25

On a cold, murky October day in 1347, a fleet of 12 Genoese trade ships sailed silently into the Sicilian harbor of Messina. Returning from the Black Sea, packed with cargo from the East, the ships would normally be beehives of activity, with sailors gathered topside, filled with anticipation to see land, reunite with family and enjoy the comforts of home.

But on that October day there was no singing, no topside celebrations, none of the usual activity associated with a much-anticipated homecoming. Instead, that afternoon a flotilla of ghost ships sailed into the Messinan harbor under a flag of silence. Though each ship's decks were filled with men, most were either dead or looked close to it, their bodies ravaged by some strange malady: Bizarre, black egglike swellings, bleeding and oozing pus, protruded from under their necks, armpits and groin areas.

Those men who still lived moaned and groaned with agonizing pain. Everything about them was detestable, not the least of which was the unbearable odor emitting from their sweating, putrid bodies. No one could stand to be in their presence for more than a few minutes. But it didn't really matter. They would all be dead within a few days.

That, history tells us, was the beginning in Europe of what later became known as the bubonic plague, commonly called the Black Death. The disease extended its deadly reach daily. Attempts to stop the plague were futile, though virtually every method was tried, including bloodletting. But the fatal scourge moved on, rapidly spreading north through Italy and ultimately to the rest of Europe and much of Asia. With tens of thousands dying and no cure or relief in the foreseeable future, people started looking for reasons for why this was happening. Was it some sort of judgment from God? Or was there another cause, one that could be traced to a more earthly source? Out of their desperation to find a scapegoat, many people identified who was to blame: the Jews.

Motivated, it was rumored, by a desire to destroy Christianity, the Jews had poisoned the water supply, thus infecting everyone—everyone except the Jews of course, who, as everyone knew, never drank from the fountains. Few Jews infected with the plague gave proof to this as the only plausible explanation. (Although other suspects were targeted as well, it was the Jewish people who received the brunt of the attacks.)

Early in 1348, a systematic extermination of Italian Jews began. Dragged from their homes, families were thrown alive into public bonfires. Others were socially and economically ostracized. Some had their property confiscated and were thrown in jail. Many were tortured before being burned at the stake. As a result of this persecution, large numbers of Jews began migrating to neighboring European countries.

As you know, the Jews had nothing whatsoever to do with the bubonic plague that threatened to wipe Europe off the map. Had superstition and paranoia not ruled popular thinking in Christendom, why so few Jews suffered from the Black Death would have been discovered: Jews refused to drink from public fountains for religious reasons (not because they had poisoned the fountains), and their strict religious dietary laws and cleansing practices coupled with their custom of living apart from mainstream society shielded them in large part from exposure to the deadly disease.

Chapter 10

A Peculiar People

Of all the people groups in recorded time, the Jews have the most colorful history. While virtually every other ancient culture has disappeared, the Jews have remained. Throughout history, they have been attacked, vilified and maligned for a variety of reasons. During the Crusades, they were hated and targeted nearly as much as Muslims. In the Middle Ages, Jews were rumored to possess magical powers given to them by the devil and they were accused of drinking the blood of Christian children after crucifying them! They were expelled from countries, overtaxed and burned by the thousands, all at the urging or direct involvement of the Church. Even Martin Luther, the great reformer, wrote a book titled *On the Jews and Their Lies*. Then there was Hitler's diabolical "final solution" to rid Germany of the Jews through racial cleansing and mass extermination. Today, we're witnessing a resurgence of anti-Semitism across the world, particularly in Europe, and this time the annihilation of the Jewish race is being called for by radical Islamic groups.

There seems to be a historical pattern here, almost like a repeating refrain. And the hook in this sad song calls for the Jewish people to simply go away. It's as if the words of Psalm 83:4 have become a theme in history: "Come . . . let us destroy them as a nation, that the name of Israel be remembered no more." But whatever new horror history throws at the Jewish people, still they will not go away.

So what's the deal with this enigmatic nation? Why are they so mysterious? And why, with a history like theirs—filled with so much war, slavery, persecution and blame—have they been able to survive with their identity intact? Why have they survived when their ancient contemporaries—the Hittites, the Amalekites and the Philistines, for instance—have largely vanished from the earth? And what does all this have to do with God?

The roots of this mystery intertwine deep below the surface, finding their genesis in Israel's unique relationship with the Creator. Embedded deep within the mystery of the Jews is that their longevity and resilience has something to do with their identity as a nation. According to the Bible, God long ago selected this people group to enjoy a special covenant relationship with Him. At first, God spoke primarily to a semi-nomadic shepherd named Abram, who lived in Mesopotamia (modern-day Iraq) about 4,000 years ago. God promised to make from Abram a great name and an even greater nation, so great that his descendants would be as numerous as the stars in the Mesopotamian night sky (see Gen. 15:1-5) With this, Abram (later called Abraham) won the equivalent of the genealogical lottery—in those days, the best thing that could happen to a man was to have a long line of descendants.

In case you haven't figured it out yet, Abraham was Jewish.

So God decided to make this promise to Abraham and to make the Jews His people. It was a simple, unconditional contract requiring only one signature: God's. And as politically incorrect as it might sound, God had this kind of relationship only with the Jewish nation. No other race or people group would enter into this particular agreement. The Jews would be God's people, yet God never intended His blessing and involvement to remain a Jewish thing alone. Through Abraham, God's plan was to bless the nations of the world through one of his descendants, specifically Jesus Christ (see Gen. 26:4).

The Jews' relationship would not be a storybook romance with the Almighty. From the very beginning, God's chosen people ran hot and cold in their relationship with God. It began with Abraham's lame attempt to jump-start God's plan by sleeping with a slave girl and having a son. That illegitimate child, Ishmael, the stepbrother of the son God promised Abraham, ultimately became the father of the Arab peoples, Israel's archenemy.

And there's been trouble in that family ever since.

Lots of Sand but No Beach

Many years later, there was a huge famine, and Abraham's family had to move where the food was: Egypt. Led at this time by Abraham's grandson Jacob, the family in Egypt were the new kids on the block, which meant they were at the bottom of the socio-economic ladder, which in turn led them into 400 years of slavery. This bondage was unexpectedly interrupted by Moses and his magic stick. After leading them across the Red Sea and stopping off at Mount Sinai to pick up the Ten Commandments, Moses and Company (about 2 million strong by this point) finally took the on-ramp to the Promised Land.

Arriving at the border, they sent an advance team to check out the cultural climate before entering. This 12-man task force returned and reported a forecast of partly cloudy with a 75-percent chance of giants raining down on their heads if they went in. Actually, 10 of the men said this, noting that this race of behemoths were so big that Israel couldn't possibly fight them. The other two guys (Joshua and Caleb) claimed that the giants' size would work in their favor—they were so big, the Israelites couldn't possibly miss them! Unfortunately, Israel had forgotten to pack their Giant-Killers Kit. Majority opinion ruled, and since they *couldn't* go back to Egypt and they *wouldn't* go into Canaan, only one option remained for them: They headed back into the desert to wander. They were stranded on the side of the road, and instead of calling for help, they just decided to stay there awhile. "Awhile" turned out to be about 40 years.

Anyway, in spite of the fact that God had previously delivered them from the most powerful army on the planet, split a river in half so that they could walk on dry ground, and provided miracle food in the desert, they nevertheless refused to trust God to save them from a few giants. Because of these trust issues, God announced that no one who was over 20 years old at the time of their Egyptian exodus would be allowed to enter the land promised to them. (In case you're wondering, that comes to about 68 funerals a day.)

Finally, after years of desert life and death, they arrived at the front gate of the land God had promised them. Once there, God has a reminder for them:

> You are a people holy to the LORD your God. The LORD your God has chosen you out of all the peoples on the face of the earth to be his people, his treasured possession.
>
> The LORD did not set his affection on you and choose you because you were more numerous than other peoples, for you were the fewest of all peoples. But it was because the LORD loved you and kept the

oath he swore to your forefathers that he brought you out with a mighty hand and redeemed you from the land of slavery, from the power of Pharaoh king of Egypt (Deut. 7:6-8).

In other words:

Remember that I picked you, not because you were the cream of the crop, but because I loved you and to keep My promise to your father, Abraham. So don't get cocky on Me, and keep in mind how powerful I am.

Just before entering the land promised to them, God warned Israel that if they disobeyed Him, there would be serious consequences (see Deut. 28). And disobey they would. Apparently suffering from a desert-induced short-term memory loss, they didn't learn the lesson from their parents' generation. Living in a neighborhood of pagan nations, it wasn't long before they stopped trusting God and began adopting the godless religious rituals of their pagan neighbors, even practicing child sacrifice (see Ezek. 16:21). So God sent some judges (spiritual and military leaders) to bail His people out of repeating cycles of sin and slavery. Ideally, He wanted to be King to His people, but they wanted to be like all the other nations and have a human king.

Bad idea.

And it proved to be a major disaster. After just three kings, the country divorced itself, splitting in half. Israel (the Northern Kingdom) got the cabin in the mountains and Judah (the Southern Kingdom) got the beach house. Then the Assyrian Mafia moved into the neighborhood and things would never be the same again. They completely scattered the Northern Kingdom. Then the Babylonians evicted the Assyrians and took Jerusalem. Now the Southern Kingdom was made into a province of the Babylonian Empire. Some of the remaining Jews fled to neighboring countries while others were forced into slave labor. Eventually, Babylon was conquered by Persia in 539 B.C. and shortly thereafter began allowing the Jews to return to their homeland. A man named Ezra helped rebuild the Temple. Jerusalem's walls were also repaired at this time, under Nehemiah's leadership.

Unfinished Business

One hundred and fifty years later, Alexander the Great showed Persia who was boss, but then he croaked and his kingdom was divided among his generals. Eventually, the Romans became king of the hill, and that, pretty much, was the score when Jesus was born.

By that time, Israel was in sad shape spiritually. Though she may have looked okay from the outside, her leaders had so twisted and perverted God's laws regarding worship that worship hardly reflected the original spirit in which it had been instituted. A fierce loyalty to tradition, a deep desire to preserve Jewish faith despite a hostile Roman occupation, and a focus on the externals of faith had blinded the Jewish religious leaders, making them deaf to what God's Spirit was saying through Jesus. By and large, the Jews didn't recognize Jesus as their promised Messiah. And in what arguably are some of the saddest words in the Bible, John writes of Jesus:

He was in the world, and the world was made through
Him, and the world did not know Him. He came to His
own, and those who were His own did not receive Him
(John 1:10-11, *NASB*).

Some Jews and Jewish leaders believed in Jesus, but the more
Jesus talked about God to His kinsmen, the more stubborn and
resistant some of them became. As a people, they flatly rejected
the One who had come to rescue them from sin (see John 1:12).

About 40 years after Jesus' resurrection, nationalistic Jews
got fed up with the Romans always telling them what to do and
they revolted, taking over control of Jerusalem. The Roman general Titus soon rode into town, destroyed the Temple, sacked
the city and restored it to Roman rule. Basically, after that happened, the Jews, without a home country, scattered throughout
the world.

Despite everything that has happened in the intervening
2,000 years, the Jews have somehow retained a core of their identity as a race and religion.

On May 14, 1948, following the century-long Zionist movement toward independence and return to their homeland, and
after winning a war intended to annihilate them, the State of
Israel was officially recognized by the United Nations.

So what about the Jewish nation today? Are they still God's
chosen people? Well, yes . . . and no.

It's like this: As far as individuals go—Jews, Asians, Latin-
Americans, Africans and Anglos (like me)—all stand as equals
and individuals before God. There are no distinctions as far as
heaven is concerned. Even among genders there are no first-

and second-class citizens (see Gal. 3:28). No matter what gender, race or ethnicity you are, God loves you unconditionally. It is *humans*, because of their sinful, selfish and controlling nature, who have created divisions, classes and categories for races and ethnic backgrounds, placing some above others. But it's not this way with God. For this reason, racism, discrimination and prejudice should have no influence in the heart of a Christian or the life of a church. Jews and Gentiles alike must believe in the Messiah in order to be heaven bound. Our Hebraic friends don't get a free pass just because they're Jewish.

But when it comes to the Jews *as a nation*, God does have some unfinished business. When Jesus came, His people officially rejected Him. Individual Jews responded to their Messiah—in fact, the vast majority of the Early Church (including the 12 apostles) was Jewish—but because of their national refusal to accept Jesus by faith as the promised Messiah, God has placed Israel on the back burner for a time while He brings Gentiles to faith (see Rom. 11:32). Paul put it this way:

> I do not want you to be ignorant of this mystery, brothers, so that you may not be conceited: Israel has experienced a hardening in part until the full number of the Gentiles has come in (Rom. 11:25).

Paul was writing primarily to non-Jewish followers of Jesus, answering the question, *Since Israel rejected God's offer of the Messiah, is He finished with them?* And the answer is a clear no. What has happened, Paul explains, is that God has allowed Israel to experience "a hardening," meaning they will continue their national blindness to Jesus as Messiah until the "fullness of the Gentiles has come in" or until all non-Jews who will trust in Christ do so (see Acts 15:14). Some believe this "fullness" will end with the Rapture, and at that time, God will once again turn His attention to the nation of Israel. And why would He do this? What's the point? Simple: God is the original Promise Keeper, and when He gives His word concerning something, He always makes good on it.

Always.

As Good as His Word

When I was in college, I had a long-distance relationship with a girl who lived about a thousand miles away. (This was in the days before cell phones, free long-distance and email.) One night about 11 P.M., my girlfriend calls and asks if I would be interested in spending the summer with her . . . in Hawaii! Now, there are things in life you pray about and there are things that are just, well . . . obvious! *Hmm . . . summer . . . paradise . . . girl of my dreams . . . yes, I'll do it!*

For three months, we lived with 50 other college students in an old mansion nestled into the side of Diamond Head Crater. In addition to honing my bodysurfing skills and developing a savage bronze tan, my love for this girl also grew that summer. It went way beyond frolicking in the Waikiki sand with her. It got to the point where I knew I *had* to be with her more than for just a summer vacation or a few hours on the phone each week. So I made the decision to transfer colleges—from the University of South Carolina to the University of Arkansas. But first, there were a few obstacles that had to be overcome, not the least of which was paying out-of-state tuition. And seeing as how my dad was covering the college bill, it ultimately became his call.

Nervously picking up the phone in the lobby of the old mansion, I placed a collect call to my dad 4,500 miles away. I don't exactly recall how I explained my reasons for wanting to transfer colleges, but I suspect Dad had already figured it out. What I do remember are his words to me: "Son, don't worry. When you get home, the money will be here."

Understand, our family didn't have much money, and I grew up in a very modest home. But there was one thing I knew about my dad, one thing I could always count on: When he said he was going to do something, he always did it. Dad was always a man of his word. That fall, I enrolled in classes at the University of Arkansas. (Oh, and that hot babe I spent the summer with on Waikiki Beach is now my awesome wife.)

Now listen to what God says to His children, Israel:

> No, I will not break my covenant; I will not take back a single word I said. I have sworn an oath to David, and in my holiness I cannot lie: his dynasty will go on forever; his throne is as secure as the sun, as eternal as the moon, my faithful witness in the sky! (Ps. 89:34-37, *NLT*).

Yahweh promised David that his heir would sit on his throne for eternity. And that promise is fulfilled in Christ. Look at what else He promised His people:

> Know . . . that the LORD your God is God; he is the faithful God, keeping his covenant of love to a thousand

generations of those who love him and keep his commands (Deut. 7:9).

Sometimes people ask me, "Is there anything God can't do?" And I typically respond with a resounding "Yes! Lots of things. He can't sin, go against His nature or go back on His word" (see Rom. 11:29) Unlike earthly parents, God is a Father who always delivers what He promises. It's an inherent, undeniable quality God possesses. He simply can't lie (see Titus 1:2).

As it relates to Israel, it appears that with all the other promises God made to them, there are still some yet-unfulfilled promises put on hold during this age of Gentile salvation and Jewish "hardening" (called "the Church Age" or "the Age of Grace" by some people). So what exactly is God going to do for Israel?

First among God's unfinished business is His promise to bring them back home to the land He originally gave them (see Deut. 30:1-3). For over 2,000 years, the Diaspora (scattered Jews) have been sown like seed across the world, living, as it were, as aliens and strangers. But the twentieth century saw huge numbers of Jews return to their homeland, especially after World War II. Some Christians believe that as the end times approach, this influx of Jews to the Holy Land will only increase.

Second, God says He will restore their hearts back to loving Him and bring judgment to Israel's enemies and all those who have persecuted them (see Deut. 30:6-7). Every nation that rises up against Israel seems to suffer a sort of curse (see Gen. 12:3). Egypt held them captive for 400 years and was cursed by God with 10 plagues; Nazi Germany tried to eradicate the Jewish race from the earth and ended up a divided country. (It would be interesting to research this topic, tracing throughout history what has happened to countries that have mistreated and persecuted the Jews.)

I'm aware that some apply these promises to a time centuries ago when Israel returned to the land following Babylonian captivity, but since that time Israel has been scattered again, mostly in Europe and the United States. I believe that all signs point to another physical return of Jews to the Holy Land and, ultimately, a spiritual restoration as well, at which time God promises to prosper Israel (see Deut. 30:8-9).

If you take God's promises literally, all the promises above remain unfulfilled. And that means God's not finished with Israel. One day He'll move her from the back burner to front and center in history. Amazing that even today, such a tiny nation somehow manages to remain in the forefront of global news. You could argue that the attention has something to do with oil or perhaps with the natural instability of the Middle East. As for me, I'm not sure how or when God will fulfill His made-long-ago promises to Israel, but I am confident He will keep His word.

And what about the rest of us, the non-Jews? This may come as a surprise, but salvation was first offered to the Jews and then to us (see Rom. 1:16). God says non-Jews (Gentiles) were like "a wild olive shoot" grafted into an existing tree (Rom. 11:17). We have been added to the covenant family of faith. Not that we were some sort of afterthought, as if God said, "Oh no! What am I going to do now that My people have rejected My Son? Hmm . . . hey, here's a thought: I'll let the Gentiles in on this deal! Great idea! Why didn't I think of that before?"

Nope. It's just that in His wisdom, God waited until His people rejected Him before turning toward us. That may not sound very equitable or politically correct, but then again, God does what pleases Him, not what fits into our understanding of fairness (see Rom. 9:14-24).

Out of Many, One

Jesus told a story once about a king who invited guests to a wedding feast for his son (see Matt. 22:1-10). But the guests ignored the invitations, saying they were too busy. They even mistreated and killed the slaves who invited them. The king became angry, instructing his remaining slaves to go out and invite whoever was willing to come so that the wedding hall would be filled with guests to honor his son.

Jesus' point was that God had invited His own people (Israel) to the salvation-wedding feast, but she rejected His offer and eventually delivered up the Bridegroom Himself to death. It was then that non-Jews received the invitation to the wedding: chosen *before* time, invited *in* time. Though Gentiles received their salvation invites after the Jews, God had already chosen them in Him before the creation of the world (see Eph. 1:4). Weird. God is everywhere, in time and out of it—in the past, present and future all at once, and mysteriously in the eternal now.

Paul says that if Israel's rejection of the Messiah brought the salvation of the Gentiles, what better things will God do when she accepts Him?!

After all, if you were cut out of an olive tree that is wild by nature, and contrary to nature were grafted into a cultivated olive tree, how much more readily will these, the natural branches, be grafted into their own olive tree! (Rom. 11:24).

God is anticipating that time when Israel once again turns their hearts toward Him in faith. The mystery of the Jews is that they didn't "get" the Messiah, yet God's not done with them. The mystery of Gentile Christians is that they "get" the Messiah, yet they don't fully understand or appreciate the Jewish roots in their Christianity. But much of the Christian faith can be understood only through embracing its Jewish roots. The mystery of the Church is that the wall between Jew and Gentile has forever been demolished through Jesus' work (see Eph. 3:6-9).

This mystery is one that has taken centuries to unfold. It's through this mystery that God tore down the dividing wall between Jew and Gentile, a barrier so thick that even the Early Church, alive with fresh faith in Jesus, struggled to accept it. As a preview of heaven and eternity, the Cross reconciled Jew and Gentile, bringing every ethnicity into the Church as one. This reality, perhaps more than any other truth in Scripture, demonstrates the reach and power of God's love. With the simple stroke of his quill, the apostle John wrote six words that ignited a fire that has burned for 2,000 years: "For God so loved the world" (John 3:16). This is what motivated God to unleash His master plan of unity and redemption for all nations, races and tribes. What humankind has never been able to achieve and what many believe Satan will attempt by establishing a one-world government and a unified Earth, God actually does through the Body of Christ.

When it comes to racial tension and social barriers in our time, we pale in comparison to the friction and hatred that existed between Jews and Gentiles at the time of Jesus. Yet through the Cross, these two seemingly irreconcilable groups are brought together. Brothers and sisters. One family. One in Christ.

* * *

The day is coming, and maybe soon, when God will reopen the file on the nation of Israel and finish what He began with her. But for now, in this parenthesis of time when Israel is on the back burner, God offers salvation to Jew and Gentile alike.

Enjoy the wedding feast.

CHAPTER 11

LINGERING QUESTIONS

MYSTERIES WE MAY NEVER SOLVE

Can you fathom the mysteries of God?

Job 11:7

Space movies fascinate me. They always have. I enjoy watching them because they challenge me to envision the future. You know: dreaming about what life will be like in the year 2525. I remember watching the classic Kubrick film *2001: A Space Odyssey* and thinking, *I have absolutely no idea what that was about.* Then *Star Wars* came along, redefining the whole sci-fi movie genre. From then on, I was hooked.

When I was a kid, our family gathered around the television to watch fuzzy images of Neil Armstrong taking his historic first steps on the moon, and it still amazes me that men traveled 240,000 miles to the moon and back. Oh sure, the geeks and engineers at NASA can explain how it was all done—using terms like "thrust," "trajectory," "apogee," "orbit," "aerobraking," "gravitational slingshot" and a host of other words and phrases that define the line between life and death for space heroes. Too much math for me, though I once entertained thoughts of becoming an astronaut when I grew up.

All that changed after I saw *Aliens*.

Outer space is still a mystery to me. Even people who study it full-time walk a fine line between fact and theory. Some stuff they're sure of, while other things keep them guessing, theorizing, pondering, postulating and wondering.

There are a ton of mysteries here on Earth that are puzzling, too—things like crop circles, Stonehenge and how those big ugly heads ended up on Easter Island. There are also a host of biblical mysteries:

• Whatever happened to the Garden of Eden?
• Will they ever find the Ark of the Covenant?

- What kind of power does Satan really have?
- Can demons possess or merely oppress Christians?
- Do demons take human form today?
- Do angels visit us today?
- Why doesn't God do the kinds of miracles He did in the Bible? Wouldn't that be a good idea in light of contemporary skepticism?
- Why doesn't God expose all the counterfeits out there who are giving Him a bad name?
- Why did God command Israel to kill innocent women and children (see Deut. 2:34; 3:6-7)? And how do we reconcile this behavior when attempting to speak up for the unborn?
- If the Church really is Christ's hands and feet, then why isn't She doing more to love Her neighbor, stand up for the oppressed, feed the starving and care for widows and orphans?

Mysteries.

One day we hope to answer these questions and solve the lingering mysteries. Then we'll be able to agree with King Nebuchadnezzar, who confessed, "Surely your God is the God of gods and the Lord of kings and a revealer of mysteries" (Dan. 2:47).

But some stuff I suppose will always be elusive. Some stuff will remain beyond our reach, certainly way above *my* head and out of *my* league. Some stuff seems so far above my understanding that I wonder, *What's the point of trying to figure it out?*

Lying in a beach chair one summer evening, I stared up into the crystal-clear night sky, trying to connect the dots, trying to figure out what's behind that little cluster of stars or what's out there beyond what my natural eyes can see. And I felt so small, lost in the wonder of the vast expanse of space.

And then I thought about my God, who is bigger than all that—bigger than what my eyes can see, bigger than our galaxy or the billions of other galaxies out there. And the amount of actual space out there—emanating out in every direction for infinity—I mean, have you ever really thought about what it really means to say that you believe in an *infinite* God? The same wall your mind hits when trying to comprehend the magnitude of outer space is the same dead end you encounter when contemplating a God who is greater than the universe itself. A God who, because of His infinitude, is much more mysterious than you or I could possibly imagine. To think that finite creatures such as us—limited by time, space, inadequate intelligence and a sin-scarred soul—could lasso the Almighty and neatly package Him inside our evangelical marketing box is absolute insanity.

I wonder if this kind of arrogance is what people react to when we tell them about Jesus. We pretend to have all the answers about God, life, relationships, problems and the dilemmas of mankind. We have nothing to learn because, well, we're Christians. And we wear our pride like perfume, convincing ourselves it makes us more attractive to God and more effective for evangelism. But what we perceive as provocative *Eau de Toilette* may actually smell more like *Eau de Toilet* to those looking for an honest, authentic connection with their Creator.

I'm aware that not everyone wants a relationship with our God and that even in our best moments we stink to some people (see 2 Cor. 2:15-16)—they simply don't want what God offers them through Jesus, and there's not much we can do about it. I get that. But though mystery may draw people to God, it's our Christian preoccupation with knowledge and answers that has driven so many away from Him. I think that we subconsciously equate knowledge with power and control. And we like to be in charge, because, after all, we have to gain the upper hand over evolutionists, liberals and secular humanists—you know, the bad guys. We've trained ourselves to defend the faith, with a special emphasis on lobbing truth grenades at the enemy while maintaining a safe distance from real, heart-to-heart contact.

But the issue is beyond just a truth-versus-lies debate. Instead of seeing people as the enemy and our answers as primary weapons, perhaps we should try another strategy—not one that ignores truth, but one that brings it to life with love. Not everyone is looking for a prepackaged or canned approach to life. We are souls, not static creatures. We are mind, emotion and will, created in God's image so that we can relate to Him in those areas. Our Father is more than merely a truth-antidote to sin. Jesus was not a truth-concept that exchanged itself for sin. He was and is Truth, the Person who died for sinners.

Clinically diagnosing a person with the sin disease, however true, isn't the only way God designed us to understand our need for a Savior. I'm not at all suggesting that we stop informing people about their identity as sinners or that we not use the word. I'm simply saying that there's more to salvation and life than lining up our beliefs and organizing them into a theological yardstick with which to measure ourselves.

That's where the mystery kicks in. We really don't have the answers for every "Why?" or "Why me?" in the world. We don't even have an answer for all our *own* questions of faith! "I don't know" may be three of the scariest words a Christian ever says, as if somehow that makes our faith weaker or less effective. But it's in our humility that others see our humble Savior more clearly (see Matt. 11:29). That's when He comes through loud and clear.

Yes, because God has left us in the dark about some things, we'll experience occasional confusion and/or frustration in our faith. As we saw in an earlier discussion, that creates tension. But faith, like relationships and life, involves tension—and friction. And if you haven't felt that in your faith yet, you're not opening your eyes and heart wide enough. Don't be afraid to go into that dark room of your house or walk down that hallway by yourself. You may not find what you're looking for there—maybe you'll end up with some loose ends and unanswered questions—but go anyway.

Real spiritual wholeness comes through embracing all God is, not just the convenient, seamless parts. And a part of Him is mystery—great mystery. That's okay. We have to allow God His secrets.

So when you look up at the night sky, realize that it bears a striking similarity to your faith: immense darkness punctuated with tiny speckles of light. Relax. It's designed to be that way.

* * *

I trust this book is a call for God-seeking people to reexamine their faith and to realize that while there is much of which we are certain, there is also mystery in virtually everything we believe. There is a time to say, "Who can know?" But our uncertainty does not breed unbelief. On the contrary, it gives birth to more faith. Not faith in a fairy tale, but confident trust as we pursue a God of history and truth. When it comes to Yahweh, there is knowledge and mystery. And intimacy can be found in both of them. Accepting the mystery means tapping into the core of Truth Himself.

Embracing these mysteries will lead you to places you'd probably rather not go, to points that intersect way above your head. And you may feel overwhelmed. You'll know Him, but not *all* of Him. You'll recognize that you may never explore all the rooms in your house of faith. You'll also understand that your faith is not now all it will be one day—but then, neither are you (see 1 Cor. 13:12). And that should give you hope.

There's a special kind of freedom you'll find in God's mysteries, a sort of release. It's that place on the map where the road ends, a place where you can hang your toes over the edge and just dream awhile.

Dream, and applaud a God that is so beyond you.

Can you fathom the mysteries of God?
Can you probe the limits of the Almighty?
They are higher than the heavens—what can you do?
They are deeper than the depths of the grave—what
can you know?
Their measure is longer than the earth
and wider than the sea (Job 11:7-9).

ABOUT THE AUTHOR

Following 17 years of immersion into America's teenage and young adult culture, Jeff Kinley transitioned his hands-on experience and founded Main Thing Ministries in 2000 (www.main thingministries.com). Main Thing's mission is to "communicate the relevancy of Christianity to this generation," and to do that, Kinley speaks to thousands each year at churches, schools, camps, retreats and seminars, and thousands more through his podcasts. He is also the founding pastor of Vintagenxt, a missional faith community in the historic Hillcrest neighborhood of Little Rock, Arkansas (www.vintagenxt.com).

Kinley is the author of 13 books, most recently *Losers Club*. He also wrote *I Can Only Imagine: Becoming the Worshipper You Long to Be* with the multi-Dove Award-winning group MercyMe, and *Through the Eyes of a Champion: The Brandon Burlsworth Story*, an inspirational story about All-American football player Brandon Burlsworth, which is currently being adapted into a major motion picture. Jeff has also written articles for several nationally known magazines, such as *Sharing the Victory*, *Men of Integrity* and *GO!*

Jeff lives in Little Rock, Arkansas, with his wife, Beverly, and three sons, Clayton, Stuart and Davis.

More Relevant Resources from Regal

A Spiritual Journey for Those Who May Have Given Up on Church But Not on God

A Place for Skeptics
Scott Larson and *Chris Mitchell*
ISBN 978.08307.37055

If you, or someone you know, are reconsidering some of the larger questions of life, then this is the book for you. This unique guidebook is a 30-day spiritual journey that examines questions about God, the Bible, faith and Jesus. *A Place for Skeptics* is written as a conversation, engaging Christian truth in a relevant, nonconfrontational style. Modern questions and doubts intersect with ancient confessions of the Christian faith in this provocative book of reflections. What results is the opportunity to consider the validity of Christianity and what it may mean to nurture and grow a real faith.

For "interested skeptics" who are not yet ready to come to church but are considering it, as well as new believers looking for something to put them on the path of regular reflection and prayer.